EGYPT
THE LAND OF THE TEMPLE BUILDERS

BY

WALTER SCOTT PERRY, M.A.

DIRECTOR OF THE SCHOOL OF FINE AND APPLIED ARTS, PRATT INSTITUTE
BROOKLYN, NEW YORK. LECTURER ON THE HISTORY OF ART
HONORARY SECRETARY OF THE EGYPT EXPLORATION FUND

THIRD EDITION

ISBN: 978-1-63923-918-4

All Rights reserved. No part of this book maybe reproduced without written permission from the publishers, except by a reviewer who may quote brief passages in a review to be printed in a newspaper or magazine.

Printed: March 2023

Published and Distributed By:
Lushena Books
607 Country Club Drive, Unit E
Bensenville, IL 60106
www.lushenabks.com

ISBN: 978-1-63923-918-4

THE PREFACE.

THE purpose in this book is to convey to the reader, through descriptive text and many illustrations, a clear, though general, idea of the art of ancient Egypt. The book is intended primarily for teachers and for students of art history, who have not time for an exhaustive study of the subject.

As an intelligent appreciation of the art of any people necessarily requires an acquaintance with their environment and civilization, the writer has brought into relief such facts as bear upon the life and religion, and the manners and customs, of this ancient people. Successive chapters trace, along evolutionary lines, the origin and development of Egyptian architecture, sculpture, painting, and decoration, as revealed by the light of modern research and personal study.

The illustrations include reproductions from carefully-selected photographs and from originals made by the author. These reproductions have been arranged with care, that they may appear opposite the pages of text they illustrate, so that the one may supplement the other.

THE CONTENTS.

Chapter.		Page.
I.	The Approach to the Pyramids	1
II.	The Pyramids of Gizeh	10
III.	The River Nile	18
IV.	Egyptian Writing	33
V.	Religion of the Ancient Egyptians	41
VI.	The Temple of Edfu	57
VII.	Thebes—The Temples of Luxor and Karnak	66
VIII.	Assuan and Philæ	97
IX.	The Temples of Denderah, Esneh, and Kom Ombo	113
X.	The Tombs of the Ancient Empire	126
XI.	The Necropolis of Thebes	161
XII.	Early Development of the Column	193
XIII.	Sculpture	210
XIV.	Temple Decoration	233
XV.	The Applied Arts	250

THE LIST OF ILLUSTRATIONS.

	Page.
MAP OF EGYPT	*Frontispiece*
ROSETTA STONE	*Frontispiece to Introduction*
ALEXANDRIA	*Frontispiece to Text*
STREET IN CAIRO	3
CAIRO: VIEW FROM THE MOKATTAM HILLS	4
ROAD TO THE PYRAMIDS	7
THE PYRAMIDS: VIEW FROM SOUTHEAST	8
THE PYRAMIDS: VIEW FROM SOUTHWEST	11
ASCENT OF THE PYRAMID OF CHEOPS	12
NILE DELTA FROM TOP OF PYRAMID OF CHEOPS	15
THE DESERT FROM TOP OF PYRAMID OF CHEOPS	16
OVERFLOW OF NILE: ASSIOUT	19
EGYPTIAN VILLAGE: KARNAK	20
PLOWING	23
METHOD OF DRAWING WATER	24
MERCHANT BOATS	27
EGYPTIAN VILLAGE NEAR LUXOR	28
MOUND FROM TOP OF THE TEMPLE OF DENDERAH	31
DENDERAH: TEMPLE AND MOUND OF ANCIENT CITY	32
TEMPLE OF DENDERAH: EXTERIOR WALL DECORATION	35
HIEROGLYPHICS: TEMPLE OF MEDINET-ABU	36
TEMPLE OF ABYDOS: RECORD OF THE KINGS OF EGYPT	39
WALL DECORATION—TEMPLE OF THOTHMES III.: KARNAK	40
WALL DECORATION—TEMPLE OF KHONSU: KARNAK	43
OSIRIS, HATHOR, AND ISIS	44
TEMPLE OF ABYDOS: WALL DECORATION	47
TOMB OF SETI I.: WALL DECORATION	48
WALL DECORATION: TEMPLE OF KOM OMBO	51
TEMPLE OF ABYDOS: WALL DECORATION IN SANCTUARY	52

THE LIST OF ILLUSTRATIONS. vii

	Page.
PYLON: KARNAK	55
LANDING ON THE RIVER BANK	56
TEMPLE OF EDFU	59
TEMPLE OF EDFU: VIEW FROM TOP OF MAIN PYLON	60
PLAN OF TEMPLE OF EDFU	63
TEMPLE OF EDFU: FIRST COURT	64
DONKEY BOY, AZER GIRCES, AT LUXOR	67
PYLONS—TEMPLE OF KHONSU: KARNAK	68
MAP OF THEBES	71
TEMPLE RUINS: KARNAK	72
TEMPLE OF LUXOR FROM THE RIVER	75
TEMPLE OF LUXOR: PYLON AND OBELISK	76
INTERIOR OF THE TEMPLE OF LUXOR	79
TEMPLE OF KHONSU: KARNAK	80
GREAT PYLON—TEMPLE OF AMMON: KARNAK	83
FIRST COURT—TEMPLE OF AMMON: KARNAK	84
GREAT HALL OF COLUMNS—TEMPLE OF AMMON: KARNAK	87
HYPOSTYLE HALL—TEMPLE OF AMMON. KARNAK	88
GRANITE SANCTUARY: KARNAK	91
WALL DECORATION: KARNAK	92
TEMPLE OF AMMON AND SACRED LAKE: KARNAK	95
ASSUAN	96
THE DESERT HIGHWAY: ASSUAN	99
OBELISK IN QUARRY: ASSUAN	100
RIVER NILE: PHILÆ IN DISTANCE	103
ISLAND OF PHILÆ	104
TEMPLES OF PHILÆ	107
HYPOSTYLE HALL—TEMPLE OF ISIS: PHILÆ	108
PHILAE: THE KIOSK	111
DENDERAH: PYLON AND TEMPLE	112
DENDERAH: MOUND OF ANCIENT CITY	115
TEMPLE OF DENDERAH: HYPOSTYLE HALL	116
SMALL TEMPLE: DENDERAH	119
TEMPLE OF ESNEH	120
TEMPLE OF KOM OMBO	123
TEMPLE OF KOM OMBO: WALL DECORATION	124
BEDRASHEN NEAR SITE OF ANCIENT MEMPHIS	127

THE LIST OF ILLUSTRATIONS.

	Page.
PYRAMID OF SAKKARAH	128
MEMPHIS: COLOSSAL STATUE OF RAMESES II.	131
STATUE OF TI: CAIRO MUSEUM	132
TEMPLE OF KOM OMBO: FOOD OFFERINGS	135
TOMB OF TI: SAKKARAH	136
TOMB OF TI: WALL DECORATION	139
PYRAMID OF CHEOPS	140
ENTRANCE TO PYRAMID OF CHEOPS	143
SECTION OF PYRAMID OF CHEOPS	144
THE SPHINX	147
TEMPLE OF THE PYRAMIDS	148
APIS TOMBS: SAKKARAH	151
SARCOPHAGUS—APIS TOMBS: SAKKARAH	152
TOMBS OF BENI-HASSAN	155
EXTERIOR OF TOMB: BENI-HASSAN	156
INTERIOR OF TOMB: BENI-HASSAN	159
LUXOR	160
DAHABIYEH ON THE NILE OPPOSITE LUXOR	163
OVERFLOW OF NILE: STATUES OF MEMNON	164
STATUES OF MEMNON	167
THE RAMESSEUM AND TOMB FIELDS	168
THE RAMESSEUM: COLOSSAL STATUE OF RAMESES II.	171
EXCAVATIONS: MEDINET-ABU	172
TEMPLE OF MEDINET-ABU	175
TEMPLE OF DER-EL-MEDINET	176
TOMB FIELDS: THEBES	179
ROAD TO TOMBS OF BIBAN-EL-MULUK	180
AT THE TOMBS OF THE KINGS: BIBAN-EL-MULUK	183
ENTRANCE TO A TOMB: BIBAN-EL-MULUK	184
TOMB OF SETI I.: BIBAN-EL-MULUK	187
UNFINISHED WALL DECORATION: TOMB OF SETI I.	188
INTERIOR OF THE TOMB OF NAKHT: THEBES	191
TEMPLE OF MEDAMUT	192
THE RAMESSEUM	195
COLUMNS: TEMPLE OF LUXOR	196
TEMPLE OF DER-EL-BAHRI	199
DER-EL-BAHRI: PROTO-DORIC COLUMNS	200

THE LIST OF ILLUSTRATIONS.

	Page.
LOTUS DECORATION: KARNAK	203
CAPITAL: PHILÆ	204
CAPITAL: **PHILÆ**	207
TEMPLE OF **PHILÆ**: EAST COLONNADE	208
STATUES OF **RA-HOTEP** AND PRINCESS **NEFERT**: CAIRO MUSEUM	211
SHEIK-EL-BELED: CAIRO MUSEUM	212
STATUE OF SCRIBE: CAIRO MUSEUM	215
SPHINXES OF HYKSOS PERIOD: CAIRO MUSEUM	216
ISIS AND HORUS: TEMPLE OF ABYDOS	219
TEMPLE OF ABYDOS: WALL DECORATION	220
SANCTUARY: ABYDOS	223
TEMPLE OF ABYDOS: WALL DECORATION	224
STATUE OF RAMESES II.: LUXOR	227
ABU-SIMBEL	228
AVENUE OF SPHINXES: KARNAK	231
TEMPLE OF EDFU: SHRINE WITHIN THE SANCTUARY	232
OFFERINGS TO OSIRIS: ABYDOS	235
JEWELS OF QUEEN AAH-HOTEP, XVIIITH DYNASTY	236
SETI I. MAKING OFFERINGS TO HORUS: KARNAK	239
TEMPLE OF EDFU: WALL DECORATION	240
HUNTING SCENE: MEDINET-ABU	243
WALL DECORATION: TOMB OF NAKHT	244
TEMPLE OF EDFU: WALL DECORATION	247
PYRAMID AND NATIVE VILLAGE	248
CHARIOT: TOMB OF IOUIYA AND TOUIYOU	251
TEMPLE OF DER-EL-BAHRI: WALL DECORATION	252
WALL DECORATION: TOMB OF SETI I.	255
MUMMY CASES: CAIRO MUSEUM	256
COUCH: TOMB OF **IOUIYA** AND **TOUIYOU**	259
COFFER: TOMB OF **IOUIYA** AND **TOUIYOU**	260
PAINTED VASES: TOMB OF IOUIYA AND TOUIYOU	263
PAINTED WOODEN BOXES: TOMB OF **IOUIYA** AND **TOUIYOU**	264
CHAIR: TOMB OF IOUIYA AND TOUIYOU	267
CEREMONIAL ROBE: BOSTON MUSEUM	268

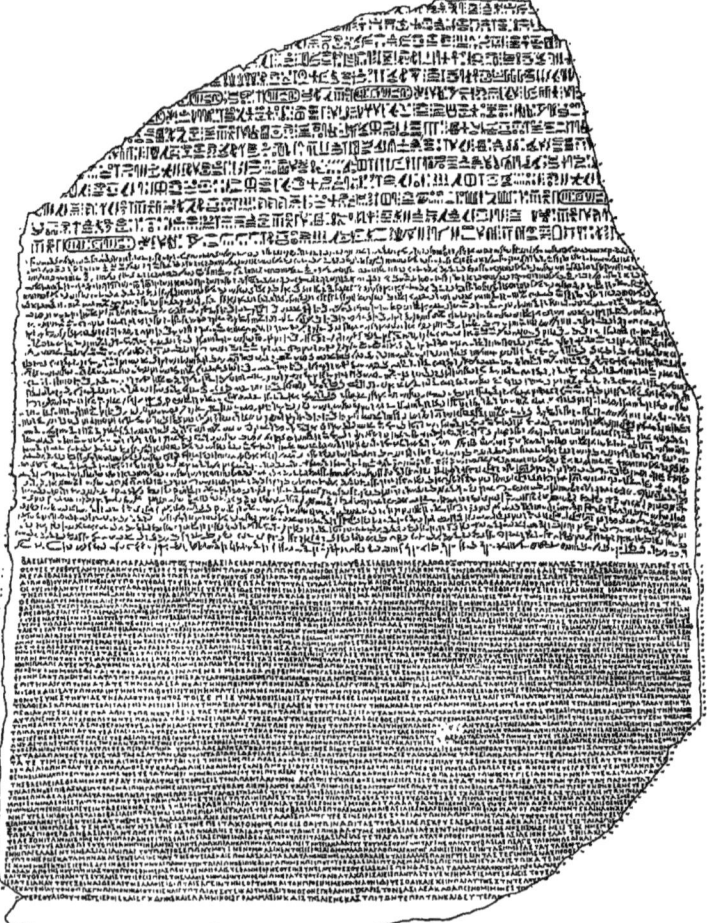

ROSETTA STONE

THE INTRODUCTION.

THE primeval history of Egypt is beyond the reach of authentic data. The old sources of information must be regarded as furnishing both fact and fiction. Manetho, an Egyptian priest of the third century before Christ, wrote a history of Egypt, fragments of which, containing lists of the early kings, still exist. Greek historians, also, have left records of their travels in that country, but modern historians must rely chiefly upon inscriptions found on architectural monuments and upon papyri. Manetho arranged the kings, or "Pharaohs," of Egypt in thirty-one dynasties covering a period of time estimated at from three to four thousand years before Christ to the time of Alexander the Great, 332 B. C. Previous to this period there was a long period of culture and civilization, known as the predynastic age. Many objects belonging to that period have been discovered. The thirty-one dynasties are divided into groups, known as the Ancient, the Middle, and the New Empires, and the Late Egyptian Period; but authors fail to agree upon the dates of these periods. Approximately, the dynasties and periods of Egyptian history are as follows:

THE INTRODUCTION.

Ancient Empire	3400 B. C. to 2200 B. C.
Dynasties I. to X. inclusive.	
Middle Empire	2200 B. C. to 1600 B. C
Dynasties XI. to XVII. inclusive.	
New Empire	1600 B. C. to 663 B. C.
Dynasties XVIII. to XXV. inclusive.	
Late Egyptian Period	663 B. C. to 332 B. C.
Dynasties XXVI. to XXXI. inclusive.	
Greek Period	332 B. C. to 30 B. C.
Roman Period	30 B. C. to 395 A. D.
Byzantine Period	395 A. D. to 640 A. D.
Mohammedan Period	640 A D. to present time.

Among the oldest monuments of Egypt are the pyramids of Gizeh, belonging to the IVth Dynasty. This and the following dynasty mark a brilliant epoch in Egyptian art. The portrait-sculpture of this very early age is remarkable for fidelity to nature and refinement of execution.

A period of several hundred years of political and religious dissension followed the Vth Dynasty and continued until the end of the Xth. Records of Egyptian history during this time are almost entirely lost.

The XIth Dynasty, marking the beginning of the Middle Empire, ushered in a period of great prosperity. The XIIth Dynasty was one of the most brilliant in the history of Egypt. It was a time of great building activity and the development of the decorative arts.

THE INTRODUCTION. xiii

The XIIIth Dynasty maintained at first the high state of civilization of the preceding, but another long era of decline was at hand. Egypt became populated with many Semitic emigrants, who in time increased in number and power, finally conquering northern Egypt. They made Tanis their capital, and their rulers are known as Hyksos or Shepherd Kings. They reigned over Egypt for many generations, adopting to some extent Egyptian customs. Under Semitic rule Egyptian art reached the darkest period in its history. The invaders were finally expelled from the country, and Egpytian supremacy was re-established during the XVIIth Dynasty, about 1600 B. C. The XVIIIth Dynasty marks the beginning of the so-called New Empire.

From the XVIIIth to the XXIst Dynasties great prosperity and wealth existed in the kingdom. It was a time of foreign conquest. The great Theban temples, the prodigious dimensions of which have been the architectural wonder of the ages, were erected. Seti I. of the XIXth Dynasty built large temples at Karnak, Kurnah, and Abydos, and the decorations of these temples and of his tomb at Biban-el-Muluk are the best of this great period of art development. His son, Rameses II., the most celebrated of Egyptian kings, showed remarkable building activity. The temples of Luxor and Abu Simbel, the Ramesseum, and temples at Karnak and Abydos are attributed to him.

But a desire to multiply works rather than to excel in their quality, with the advent of a too bounteous symbolism, eventually led to an inevitable downfall in art. Sculpture became conventional in style. Under Rameses III. of the XXth Dynasty, building continued; with the close of this dynasty, however, in 950 B. C., the empire again fell to pieces: Thebes gave way to Tanis, the capital, during the XXIst Dynasty; and, under the following dynasty, Bubastis became the royal residence. Small independent principalities followed and, in 722 B. C., Egypt was governed by the Ethiopians, only to become, later, subject to the Assyrians. The foreign power at last being overthrown, Egypt became reunited and a new period of prosperity was established.

The brightest part of this new or Renaissance period is covered by the XXVIth Dynasty, dating from 663 B. C. to the Persian conquest, 525 B. C. In 332 B. C., Egypt fell into the hands of the Greeks, who, ruling the country until thirty-two years before Christ, made it a kingdom of great prosperity, at the same time respecting the customs and religion of the Egyptians. The Ptolemaic period was followed in 30 B. C. by the Roman. The Romans also sought to encourage the art of the Egyptians. Christianity was early introduced and the edict of Theodosius the Great gave a final blow to paganism. After the division of the Roman Empire, 395 A. D., the Byzantines controlled Egypt until

640 A. D., when the all-conquering Mohammedans took possession; they still share supremacy under the rule of Great Britain.

Thus have the nations of men followed one another in gradual succession as they have taken possession of the fertile valley of the Nile. And as in the olden times men flocked thither to draw from the storehouse of the world's granary, so to-day they burrow among the ruins of her once-glorious temples and tombs for the art treasures that are still her own.* All nations, directly or indirectly, have borrowed from Egypt of her arts and sciences, readapting them to meet new conditions. In studying the evolution of art, we must begin with Egypt and trace its embryonic life in her unrecorded past. If all nations owe to Egypt something of their art-idea, to whom, in turn, is she indebted? That question may forever remain unanswered; but true it is that in the earliest times of which man has any record, Egypt had reached a high state of civilization, and equally true is it that her arts have culminated in the more perfect arts of the modern world.

---
*Among other explorers and societies the Egypt Exploration Fund, with headquarters in England and the United States, has been the means of many remarkable discoveries that have greatly enriched the museums

ALEXANDRIA

EGYPT:

The Land of the Temple Builders.

I.

THE APPROACH TO THE PYRAMIDS.

MORE than three thousand miles of ocean rolls between the port of New York and the Rock of Gibraltar, that " Pillar of Hercules," guarding, like a crouching lion, the great Mediterranean. A fitting sentinel it is for a sea which, washing the shores of Europe, Asia, and Africa, is bounded by a territory where have been enacted so many important events in the great drama of the world's civilization.

Nine hundred and twenty miles farther eastward and Vesuvius cuts the horizon, its column of smoke brilliant in color before the rising sun. Southeastward are the Lipari Islands, where the volcanic cone of Stromboli — the ancient abode of Æolus, wind-god of the Greeks — rises abruptly from the sea; and, farther on, by way of the Strait of Messina, Mount Etna is seen raising her lofty head and reddening the sky before the sinking sun. Somewhat over a thousand miles from Naples, the traveller looks out upon the low, level shore that marks the approach to the Nile country. Across the delta, one hundred and thirty miles farther, is Cairo, the gateway to the land of the great temple-builders of ancient Egypt.

This city, belonging to the Turkish Empire and containing fully half a million inhabitants, is situated at the upper angle of the Nile delta, which stretches its triangular form northward to the Mediterranean. Perhaps in no other place can be found a greater variety of pronounced racial types than is encountered in this cosmopolitan city of the East, where are seen people differing so widely in costume, in history, in thought, and in religion. The majority of the population consists of Turks and Arabs, the former occupying situations as government officials, soldiers, and tradesmen, while the latter fulfil the duties of servants, donkey-boys, and shop-keepers. In addi-

STREET IN CAIRO

CAIRO: VIEW FROM THE MOKATTAM HILLS

tion, Europeans and Orientals from many regions, native Fellahs and Copts, Algerians, Moors, Jews, Negroes, — with a few resident, and many tourist, Americans, — all contribute to form an extraordinarily mixed population.

The eastern or older quarter of the town affords opportunity to study the many phases of oriental life; for it is here that the people carry on their different trades and occupations. Here the streets are not only ill-paved, but too narrow to admit an ordinary carriage. Men, women, children, and animals jostle one another in the crowded thoroughfares; and the noisy cries of venders, shop-keepers, and money-changers, mingled with the braying of donkeys, increase the confusion.

What offends the ear, however, is forgiven by the eye, in the feast of color that greets it on every side. Gay oriental stuffs, beautiful rugs and prayer-carpets, shining brass and copper vessels, as well as gold, silver, and tinsel ornaments, are heaped about in picturesque disorder. Countless little shops are supplied with all sorts of articles arranged to attract the purchaser.

6   THE LAND OF THE TEMPLE BUILDERS.

The proprietor — seated cross-legged upon his rug-covered platform and within easy reach of his goods — loses no chance of importuning all passers-by to a close inspection of his wares. Above the shops are the balconies and latticed windows of the domestic quarters, which cut off from the gaze of the European the domestic life of the Mohammedan.

Through these crowded streets, one threads his way to the plateau surmounting the Mokattam hills at the east of the town, whence may be gained a good idea of the appearance of the delta, the Nile valley, and the desert. The city lies stretched out at the feet of the observer, a mass of flat-roofed buildings, out of which, here and there, spring in clear relief the minarets of Mohammedan mosques. Beyond flows the Nile through fields of ripening grain, its surface dotted with the lateen sails of picturesque merchant-boats. Farther on, at the edge of the desert, rise the wonderful pyramids of Gizeh, glistening in the sun and piercing the sky with their immutable crests.

From Cairo a well-constructed road shaded by

ROAD TO THE PYRAMIDS

THE PYRAMIDS: VIEW FROM SOUTHEAST

fine lebbek trees leads to these pyramids. The trip may be made by carriage in an hour and a half. The road spans the Nile by a long iron bridge and extends along the angle of the delta to the desert. The pyramids stand upon the edge of the desert on the western bank of the Nile, almost opposite the point where the river divides into its many mouths or outlets.

At first the apparent size and distance of the three great pyramids are most deceptive. Being the only prominent objects in the landscape, they seem very near, when in fact they are several miles away. Upon approaching them, they appear to increase rapidly in size and their grouping and relationship change much with the observer's point of view. From the road, the two smaller pyramids are partly hidden by the great Cheops, creating the supposition that the bases of all three are in proximity to one another. From a point more nearly opposite, one is surprised to find how far apart they are in reality. A view from the southwest will bring them again so near to one another in appearance that their bases seem to overlap.

II.

THE PYRAMIDS OF GIZEH.

IT must be borne in mind that, while especial interest centres in the three great pyramids, there are many more of these massive burial vaults, both near the necropolis of the ancient city of Memphis and scattered along the plateau of the Libyan desert for a distance of twenty-five miles.

The sides of the three great pyramids of Gizeh — Cheops, Chephren, and Mycerinus — face the four cardinal points of the compass. Cheops measures, approximately, seven hundred and fifty feet on each of the four sides. It is four hundred and fifty feet in height and covers an area of nearly thirteen acres. Its estimated weight is about seven million tons. Let one consider any ground-area of thirteen acres of land with which he is familiar, and in imagination pile upon it, in pyramidal order, blocks of stone with

THE PYRAMIDS: VIEW FROM SOUTHWEST

ASCENT OF THE PYRAMID OF CHEOPS

an average thickness of three feet, until the apex shall reach a point four hundred and fifty feet from the foundation, and he will then have gained some idea of the colossal dimensions of this silent witness of more than five thousand years of human life and activity.

The first requirement for the actual construction of the pyramid appears to have been the levelling of the rock surface. This was probably followed by the excavation of the subterranean chambers and the building of a foundation of stone reaching up to the level of the surrounding sands. This foundation was then covered with a layer of stones about three feet thick. Stones for another similar layer were rolled up an incline of earth and put in place. Then other layers were added till the top was reached. The incline of earth was raised as needed for each platform and when all were in place the earth was removed. Thus the great pyramids may have reached their gigantic proportions. The summit was crowned with a pyramidal stone and the step-like spaces on the surface were filled so as to form a solid mass with four sloping sides. As in due course of time this surface covering has disappeared, the summit is now accessible. But to climb to the top of one of these pyramids, under any circumstances, is no easy matter; for the true steepness is not measured by the slant of the long lines from the angles of the base to the apex, — as seen in the illustration, — but by the slope of the outline presented by a face view.

The ascent is made upon one of the four sides, over steps or blocks of stone averaging at least three feet in height. Even with two or three Arab attendants the task is more than many travellers can endure in the hot tropical sun. The ambitious climber must rest often before he reaches the top. Yet he is amply repaid for his trouble. Looking off to the north and northeast, he sees spread before him the great delta of the Nile, extending far into the distance until it is lost in the northern horizon. Level as a floor, and dotted with small villages, this great arable tract is covered a large part of the year with a rich vegetation. Its soil, formed from the alluvial deposits of the river, yields an abundant harvest to the inhabitants, but unfortunately subjects

NILE DELTA FROM TOP OF **PYRAMID OF CHEOPS**

THE DESERT FROM TOP OF PYRAMID OF CHEOPS

them to the baneful influences of a malarial atmosphere.

To the south is the river Nile, hemmed in by the Arabian desert on the east and the Libyan desert on the west, the fertile soil on both sides varying in width from a few hundred feet to several miles; and beyond is the great sea of drifting sands. East of the middle pyramid and in the immediate foreground, the mysterious figure of the Sphinx, sculptured from the solid rock and partly buried in the sands and the dust of ages, looks toward the rising sun.

Turning toward the west and southwest, one views a scene strikingly unlike that of the luxuriant fields bordering the river. Here all is desolation and dreary waste. The yellow-brown drifting sand shining under the glare of the noon-day sun, interspersed with barren rocks and dotted here and there with the crumbling remains of ancient tombs, is the very antithesis of the scene just beheld. The pyramids, built as tombs for the rulers of the IVth Dynasty, mark in the landscape the dividing line between life and death.

III.

THE RIVER NILE.

THE town of Assuan, situated at the first cataract. five hundred and eighty miles by river from Cairo, is one of the chief points of destination for all pilgrimages through the Nile valley. The trip to Assuan and back to Cairo may be made by an excursion steamer in three weeks, allowing for short visits to the various places of interest; but a more ideal journey may be tàken in the picturesque sail-boat peculiar to the Nile and known as the dahabiyeh. The latter is a slow mode of travel governed entirely by winds, and consumes many weeks, but contributes more than a shorter voyage toward a full comprehension of the character of the life along the river.

Little wonder that to the ancient Egyptians the river Nile was a mystery they regarded with a feeling of reverence, believing that a god dwelt within its waters! For many hundred miles

OVERFLOW OF NILE: ASSIOUT

EGYPTIAN VILLAGE: KARNAK

from the mouth, no tributary breaks its winding outline. Onward it flows through rainless regions beneath an almost tropical sun, spreading abroad the fertile bounty which, for untold centuries, made Egypt the granary of the world. Tens of thousands of people still dwell upon its productive banks, drawing daily from its fountain of waters for purposes of irrigation and domestic consumption. Seemingly the river grows wider and deeper as it makes its way toward the Mediterranean, although it actually loses one-third its volume. Every year, beginning in June, it slowly fills its bed between the steep alluvial banks, and then as deliberately spreads its turbid waters over the rich soil to the desert's edge. Having deposited its freight of vitalized earth, its mission accomplished, it gradually recedes; and, reaching its winding bed, again sinks many feet below the level surface of the land.

The mean difference between the highest and lowest level of the river is thirty-eight feet at Thebes, twenty-five feet at Cairo, and five feet in the delta. The annual overflow of the Nile no longer turns its valley into a great lake, as it must have done in earlier times; for, through engineering skill, man now controls, to a certain extent, the waters of the river. By means of canals and embankments, these waters are conducted to various parts of the Nile valley, to be utilized according to agricultural requirements. The canals are sufficiently deep to supply somewhat remote districts with water during the dry season.

The productive soil left by the retreating Nile requires but the merest scratching of its yielding surface by the primitive plough to be made ready for the seed. Owing, however, to the absence of rain, the crops must be watered continually by artificial means; therefore, throughout the long days, hundreds of native workmen draw water from the river and raise it to the little canals, which, like the lines of a checkerboard, divide the arable land.

The water is lifted from the river by means of a shadoof. This rude apparatus consists of a long pole like a well-sweep, with a bucket at one end and a ball of dried mud as a weight at the other. When the river is low, a man stationed

PLOWING

METHOD OF DRAWING WATER

at the water's edge fills the vessel, raises it with his shadoof, and pours the water into a hole in the embankment above him. Other men above, each with a shadoof, successively dip and lift the water upward until the top of the embankment is reached. By a network of little canals, the water is conducted over a tract of cultivated soil. When this has been well watered, the supply is shut off by banking the main channel with earth, and the water directed to another part of the field. This process is continued until the entire tract has received its supply. Week after week this operation is repeated, furnishing employment to many men, who receive from ten to fifteen cents per day for their labor. Wells also are dug here and there, into which water percolates from the river. This water is drawn by means of a large wheel, to the rim of which are suspended earthen jars. The wheel is turned by another of rude gearing; to this is attached some animal, usually a buffalo, which slowly performs his part in furnishing the necessary motor power to set the wheels in motion.

The life along the river is unique and interesting. Flat-bottomed boats, freighted with merchandise brought by camels across the desert to Assuan, float lazily down the river, now and then catching a favoring wind and speeding swiftly round the curves, their sails, like the wings of gigantic birds, silhouetted against the level shores and clear sky. Here and there along the banks may be seen women filling their water-jars or standing in picturesque groups with their dripping burdens resting upon their heads. In place of earthen jars, the men use the skin of an animal, which they hang upon their backs. Thus do these primitive people carry to their rude dwellings, for domestic purposes, the water of the Nile — not crystalline and clear like that of a spring, but freighted with the black mud of the river.

But how do these natives build their houses and what is the character of their homes? Grouped beneath the palm-trees, one finds irregular structures consisting of walls built of Nile mud or of sun-dried bricks, and rising to a height of six to eight feet. They are divided from one another by crooked lanes, which intersect the

MERCHANT BOATS

EGYPTIAN VILLAGE NEAR LUXOR

crowded settlement. Within the walls of such a dwelling lives the Egyptian of to-day, with his wife and children, in close companionship with his donkeys, his dogs, and his pigeons. Sometimes a part of the enclosure is divided into compartments or rooms, a few feet square, and is topped with a roof of straw. Scarcely an article of furniture redeems these comfortless dwellings. A raised platform of dried mud may form the bed for the master of the house; a hemispherical mound of earth with openings, the crude stove. The latter is rarely in use, as the bread is baked at the public bakery whenever the family supply runs low. There is little wood; the village refuse takes the place of fuel. An accumulation of dust several inches deep carpets the ground.

Most of the village houses along the Nile are of this mud formation. In Cairo and in other large towns are buildings similar to those of European construction; but, outside of these few cities, the greater proportion of the natives that inhabit the Nile country dwell with their animals in the most primitive mud structures.

If one understands the construction of the

Egyptian dwelling of to day, he may more readily comprehend the origin of the mounds that cover the sites of ancient cities and oftentimes surround a temple, in some cases rising to a height varying from fifty to seventy feet. If the ancient Egyptian house crumbled to the extent of being uninhabitable, the *débris* was levelled and another habitation erected upon the same spot. Thus, through countless ages, the city gradually increased the height of its level above the river until it encircled the great temple. In later centuries, when the Egyptians cared not for the religion of their fathers, the temples were used as dwelling-places and in time became filled, and even covered, with accumulations from the ruins of many habitations.

The excavations of these mounds have brought to light not only countless hieroglyphic inscriptions upon temple walls and upon papyrus rolls, but long-buried household utensils and trinkets in great numbers. They have rediscovered Egypt to us, in that we are able to form from them a clear conception of the history and life of the ancient Egyptians.

MOUND FROM TOP OF THE TEMPLE OF DENDERAH

DENDERAH: TEMPLE AND MOUND OF ANCIENT CITY

IV.

EGYPTIAN WRITING.

THE inscriptions upon the temple walls and upon papyrus rolls show that the Egyptians employed three kinds of writing. The first, or oldest form, the hieroglyphic, is largely pictorial in character. Figures of men, birds, animals, and material objects are combined with various symbols. This form was usually adopted for temple writings.

A more facile method naturally came about through the abbreviation of the original outline or pictorial symbol. That is, a part of the representation was used to symbolize a whole character. For instance, two curves combined somewhat like the figure *3* replace the early hieroglyphic drawing of the owl. This form of writing is known as the hieratic, and much of the writing upon papyrus is of this character.

These two forms of writing became still further

modified and abbreviated until the original pictorial form was almost entirely lost. One simple character, composed of a line only, came to stand for the original symbol. This style of writing was in use at least one thousand years before Christ, and was largely employed in commercial transactions, in correspondence, and in making contracts. It is known as the demotic.

In the early centuries after Christ, a combination of the demotic and the Greek, known as the Coptic, became common. A large proportion of the Coptic writings that have been preserved are of a religious character, many containing parts of the Old and of the New Testament.

Happily, a clew to the reading of these writings came about through the discovery at Rosetta, in 1799, of a fragment of a black basalt slab measuring about two and one-half by four feet. On one face of this stone are three inscriptions: one in hieroglyphic, another in demotic, and a third in Greek. The translation of the Greek text explained the purpose of the writing and also the fact that the same law was proclaimed in the three inscriptions. Through a series of years, scholars

TEMPLE OF DENDERAH: EXTERIOR WALL DECORATION

HIEROGLYPHICS: TEMPLE OF MEDINET-ABU

gave careful study to these characters and finally succeeded in deciphering the whole Egyptian alphabet, thus rendering intelligible the innumerable inscriptions found on the Egyptian temples and tombs.

The chief credit for this work is due Jean François Champollion, although his work has been supplemented by that of many other students. While Egyptian inscriptions may now be translated quite easily by Egyptologists, it should be remembered that, to acquire this facility, careful and untiring research and study were necessary; for, in their writings, the Egyptians employed a great many signs—fully two thousand in number. These arbitrary symbols were often supplemented by pictorial forms, that the meaning might be more easily determined. An elliptical ring or cartouche containing characters signifies the name of a king; although, occasionally, an inscription thus enclosed in an elongated space with rounded ends has reference to the gods. An inscription consisting entirely of these cartouches and cut in low relief upon a high wall among the ruins of Abydos, gives a partial chronological record of the kings of

Egypt from the time of Menes. This record is of great value, inasmuch as it verifies in point of time the reigns of the successive Egyptian kings referred to in various inscriptions found throughout Egypt.

The atmospheric conditions of this rainless country—with its cloudless sky, its wide stretches of desert, and its tropical sun—have always been favorable to the preservation of the works of man. Drawings, carvings, paintings, and inscriptions, made on stone from one to three thousand years before Christ, are nearly as perfect to-day as when wrought by the Egyptian draughtsman. The hand of man, however, has proved more destructive to these records of countless generations than the forces of nature. The Assyrians, the Persians, the Mohammedans, and the disinterested natives have in turn played their part in the demolition of temples and works of art. Yet the visitor is amazed at the number, the clever workmanship, and the splendor of those which remain scattered throughout Egypt.

TEMPLE OF ABYDOS: RECORD OF THE KINGS OF EGYPT

WALL DECORATION — TEMPLE OF THOTHMES III: KARNAK

V.

RELIGION OF THE ANCIENT EGYPTIANS.

THE religion of the ancient Egyptians is of a most interesting as well as complex character, differing throughout the empire with locality and period of time. The Egyptians saw divine power in everything, and divine attributes were usually given a personal form. These personal forms were provided with a symbolic head-dress, or were sometimes represented with the head of a beast or bird, to signify their rank among the gods and their relationship to supernatural powers. Ptah, the greatest of the gods, was the divine source of creative power, and was represented in human form with the body swathed as a mummy. Ra, the god of the sun, who illumines the world, ranked next to Ptah. He was given human form with a hawk's head, and wore a sun-disk and the Uræus serpent. Hathor, the mother-god, a divine source of creative power, wore the vulture cap, and was sometimes crowned with the horns of the cow and with the disk.

In a country like Egypt, the sun, seemingly rising directly out of the desert, travelling all day without a cloud to darken its face, and sinking at night into the sands of the western horizon, produces upon one an effect quite different from that experienced in northern latitudes, where, in a rainy season, it may be lost to view for many days at a time. No wonder the Egyptians made it an object of vital significance and worship. They could not comprehend its mysterious power; they felt that through the night it wrestled with the unseen god of darkness and, though vanquished, lived again. In the morning the sun-god rose as a child, Horus; at mid-day it was the god Ra in the zenith of strength; and at night, the old man Tum, going down to repeat the conflict with the god of evil. Thus the sun became the symbol of resurrection; though dying at night, it was revitalized through the resources of nature which were presided over by the goddess Isis.

WALL DECORATION — TEMPLE OF KHONSU: KARNAK

OSIRIS, HATHOR, AND ISIS

One trinity of the Egyptian gods consisted of Osiris, Isis and Horus. Osiris, the principle of light, lost his life through conflict with Typhon, the god of darkness. When Horus or Ra is spoken of as the soul of light, it signifies that he is the son of Osiris and renders visible the hidden element of light. According to some forms of Egyptian belief, Osiris is represented as the ruler of the dark regions and the judge of souls. A person dying without sin, or having undergone a period of purification, was permitted to unite with the soul of Osiris. Osiris is represented with a human head, and he is either in the form of a mummy or seated upon a throne. He is decorated with the ostrich feathers of truth.

Hathor and Muth are other names for Isis, the three having much the same significance and representing the female principle of life.

Anubis was the guide of the dead through the dark regions of Hades. It was his function to preside over funeral rites and to guard the kingdom of the west or the setting sun, the land beyond the grave. He was represented with the head of a jackal.

Ammon-Ra, the great god of Upper Egypt, the god of Thebes, whose name signified the Hidden One, was a deity of later origin. Attributes of nearly all the gods of Egypt became impersonated in this one god Ammon-Ra. Every god was subordinate to the great and mysterious Ammon. He was usually represented as enthroned or standing, adorned with a long headdress with royal insignia. In his hand he carried a sceptre, a scourge, and the key of life.

No other ancient people had so absolute faith in resurrection and in the immortality of the soul as did the early Egyptians. They believed in a future state of punishment and of reward, although the thought regarding the life of the soul after the death of the body was not the same at all times and in all parts of Egypt. Because of this belief in the life of the spirit and its return to the body at some future time, everything possible was done to guard against the annihilation of the body. It was not only embalmed and preserved in the form known to us as the Egyptian mummy, but placed in a massive tomb constructed for its reception and safe-keeping. In

TEMPLE OF ABYDOS: WALL DECORATION

TOMB OF SETI I.. WALL DECORATION

RELIGION OF THE ANCIENT EGYPTIANS. 49

the early periods of history, statues portraying the likeness of the individual were buried within the walls of the tomb, that the spirit, after undergoing purification and returning to earth, might recognize its own image in case the body should be destroyed. This belief had great influence upon portrait-sculpture, as will be seen in subsequent chapters.

According to the belief of the Egyptians, every individual consisted of three or more parts: the body, belonging to this world; the soul, actually belonging to another world to which it would ultimately return; and the divine intelligence. When the soul was released from the body, it was thought to undergo trials corresponding to the moral life of the individual when on earth. To give support in these trials, texts and inscriptions upon papyrus, as well as amulets, were preserved with the mummy. At length the heart was weighed in the scales of justice and balanced by the god of truth. The god Anubis superintended the weighing, and sentence was pronounced by the counsellors of the gods. If the heart were found perfect, the soul was restored by Osiris to the mummy. Erring souls were to suffer punishment, or they might enter the bodies of animals, to begin life anew.

The divine spirit, the third part of the human life, became united with the sun-god Ra, and with him traversed the heavens in his golden boat or walked the earth with the living. In course of time it was supposed that the divine intelligence, the soul, and the body or mummy would become reunited.

Many were the symbols employed by the Egyptians in giving expression to these religious beliefs. The hawk upon the head of Horus was symbolic of the flight of that bird toward the sun. The scarabæus laid its egg and, enclosing it in a little ball of mud, placed it out of reach of the waters of the Nile. The Egyptian knew not that the ball enclosed an egg; to him, out of the earth came a new life, consequently the scarabæus became a sacred symbol of rebirth, resurrection, and eternal life. Beside being a symbol of immortality, it was emblematic of creative power. Scarabs reproduced in stone, gold, ivory, wood, paste and potter's clay were used as amulets for the

WALL DECORATION: TEMPLE OF KOM OMBO

TEMPLE OF ABYDOS: WALL DECORATION IN SANCTUARY

living and the dead. They were buried with the mummy in large numbers; those one or more inches long were placed over the heart. So placed, it was believed that they would assist in driving away evil spirits during the transmigration stage. And, as in the resurrection the heart would be the first to receive vitality, the scarab, as the sacred symbol of rebirth, would be of great significance. In the Book of the Dead, a copy of which was often buried with the mummy, are found the words: "My heart that comes to me from my mother, my heart that is necessary to me for my transformation." Other passages of great interest recall parts of the Hebrew Scriptures; for instance, we read in the translation: "I have given bread to the hungry; I have given water to the thirsty; I have given clothes to the naked." The scarabæus was especially sacred to the god Ammon-Ra. It was so much allied to the worship of the sun that it was often represented with the sun's disk. It was frequently employed in decoration, and in the hieroglyphic writings, to signify "To be, to become, to raise up."

The Egyptian evidently did not associate death

and the tomb with unmitigated horror. In many pictures found upon the monuments, the departing soul is represented as being transferred in a boat across the river. Upon the boat is pictured the tomb, its doorway almost completely covered by a sail, which is the symbol of coming breath or renewed life.

The winged sun-disk is also a most interesting symbol. It was placed over doorways, and upon the lintels of passageways and entrance pylons. The outspread wings were emblematic of divine protective power. On both sides of the disk appears the Uræus serpent, to signify royalty.

The lotus is one of the most typical features in Egyptian decoration. It is represented in every imaginable form of outline from the bud to the full blossom. It is a symbol of resurrection and of immortality.

Such use of symbols we find in modified form in early Christian art. The fish is emblematic of Christ, the dove, of the Holy Spirit, and the cock, of Christian watchfulness; while the four Evangelists were often represented by the angel, the lion, the ox, and the eagle.

PYLON: KARNAK

LANDING ON THE RIVER BANK

VI.

THE TEMPLE OF EDFU.

EDFU, five hundred miles above Cairo, is not the first temple reached on the river voyage, but its almost perfect state of preservation and simplicity of plan make it the best example with which to begin the study of temple construction.

When a halt in the Nile voyage is made to visit the temple of Edfu,—as is the case in visiting any town, temple, or tomb along the river,— the steamer is no sooner moored to the river bank than it is immediately besieged by hundreds of clamoring Arabs, who fight desperately for the saddles as they are passed ashore from the boat, that they may gain passengers for their donkeys. These "donkey-boys"—often in reality full-grown men—follow close at the heels of the little animals and provoke them into a trot by frequent applications of the whip or by occasional twists of the tail, adding discomfort not only to the beast but to the rider.

Despite this somewhat unreliable means of progress, the temple is soon reached, as it is but a short distance from the river. It is surrounded by the *débris* of ancient cities; in fact, it was almost completely covered with the accumulations of many centuries until 1860, when it was thoroughly excavated. It is in an almost perfect state of preservation, although two thousand years have passed since it was reconstructed. In all probability its foundation dates back to a very early period. Its walls are covered with most interesting inscriptions, from which we learn that restorations were commenced two hundred and thirty-five years before Christ and finished one hundred years later. The temple is dedicated to the god Horus, " Horus who spreads his wings; the great god; the lord of heaven, who, clad in bright plumage, comes forth out of the sun-mountain." When the temple was consecrated, an image of the god was carried in solemn procession; and extended accounts are given of the elaborate festivals that were held in honor of the god at the completion of the temple. According to the inscriptions, Horus

TEMPLE OF EDFU

TEMPLE OF EDFU: VIEW FROM TOP OF MAIN PYLON

THE TEMPLE OF EDFU. 61

is astonished at the magnificence of the building and joyfully expresses himself in words of praise. Full accounts are given of the process of its erection. Definite specifications relate to every detail of construction, including the decoration of the walls with gold and many colors.

As one approaches Edfu, the pylon looms up above the great mound of earth at its base. This pylon or gateway is over two hundred and fifty feet wide and one hundred and fifteen feet high. The top may be reached by a staircase of two hundred and forty steps. From this point is gained a very good idea of the surrounding country, of the Nile, and of the villages, as well as of the ground plan of the building, which, including the pylon gateway with interior court, is four hundred and fifty feet long and two hundred and fifty feet wide.

Originally, the Egyptian temple probably consisted of the sanctuary only—a building of four walls; and in the construction of any Egyptian temple the sanctuary was the nucleus or part first built. In the desire to produce a temple of more impressive appearance and to provide chambers necessary for the preservation of relics used in religious ceremonies, the building was gradually extended outward, the successive erections increasing in width and height toward the great entrance or pylon at the front, until many pylons and walls divided the interior courts or halls from one another. Thus, in the temple of Edfu, we find a huge pylon with high towers, then a large forecourt surrounded by a high wall and colonnade. Back of this court is a hypostyle or pillared hall, the roof being supported by eighteen columns. Successive doorways give admission to smaller and darker halls, leading to the sanctuary in which was placed the image of the god.

The various chambers of the temple are dimly lighted by slight openings in the roof, and even to-day there lingers an atmosphere of mystery and awe. One steps reluctantly into this pagan temple, as if trespassing upon forbidden ground. Nevertheless, one is not content till he has penetrated into its sanctuary, within which is to be seen a beautiful shrine of granite such as is not often found in Egyptian temples. Owing to the destruction of a part of the roof, this otherwise

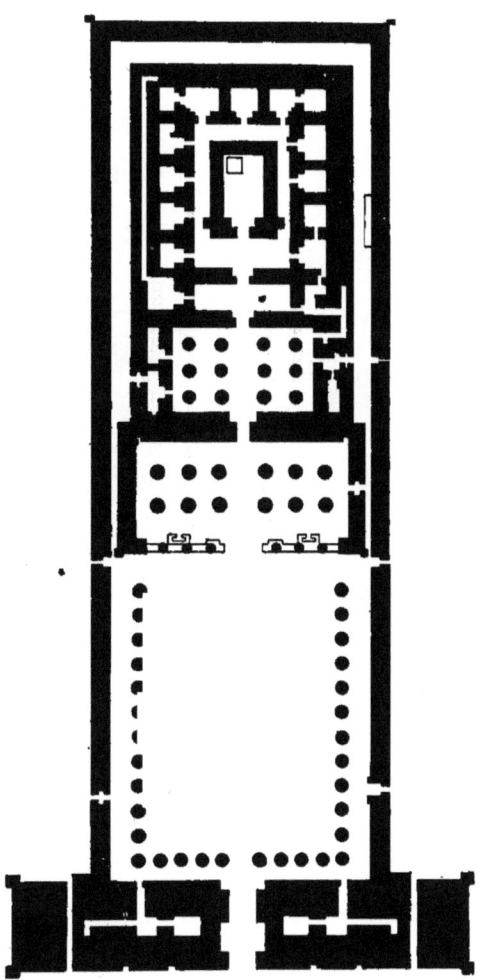

PLAN OF TEMPLE OF EDFU

TEMPLE OF EDFU: FIRST COURT

perfectly dark chamber and its inscriptions may be easily studied.

Upon the walls of the temple are inscriptions, drawings, figures of gods and kings; and when all these decorations were brilliant in color and the temple was perfect in its construction, the sight must have indeed stirred the soul of the worshipper. From the masts placed in front of the pylons floated pennants, and gorgeous processions moved slowly and impressively toward the great temple on festive days, bearing standards of color, symbols, and images of the gods.

All, however, were not admitted to the sacred temple. Some were permitted to step within the first court; a more privileged few might pass within the second hall; only the elect entered the third court; and, to the "holy of holies," only the high priest and the king, who represented the god on earth, were admitted.

VII.

THEBES: THE TEMPLES OF LUXOR AND KARNAK.

How glorious was ancient Thebes when the great kings of the XVIIIth and XIXth Dynasties ruled in Upper Egypt, when the greatest temples the world has ever seen had been erected upon the eastern bank of the river, when magnificent memorial chapels on the opposite shore marked the city of the dead, and sacerdotal processions wended their way through the city and between rows of silent sphinxes to the temple gates!

The foundation of Thebes may date back more than two thousand years before Christ, but the time of its great prosperity was after the city of Memphis had lost its supremacy. The temples of the gods were erected during the reigns of Amenhotep, Thothmes, Hatasu, Seti I., and Rameses the Great.

DONKEY BOY, AZER GIRGES, AT LUXOR

PYLONS — TEMPLE OF KHONSU: KARNAK

In this city was supposed to dwell the great god Ammon, with whom was associated Ra of Lower Egypt; together they were known as Ammon-Ra. In Ammon's honor was erected the gigantic temple of Karnak, the largest in the world, the wonder of the ages. Great wealth was bestowed upon this god. Distinguished men of the kingdom served as his priests. Thebes was a city of triumph, of wealth, and of learning, and increased not only in splendor and power, but also in the magnificence of its temple worship. In time its fame became known to the Persians and the Greeks. Cambyses and his army succeeded in reaching Upper Egypt, but, fighting in sight of the temples of Ammon, the Egyptians were able to withstand the assault. In honor of their triumph and in gratitude for the aid rendered by their god, they added other pylons to the Theban temples.

In the brilliant period of Greek civilization, Thebes must still have been a great city, although it had departed from the zenith of its former splendor. Extravagant and unworthy rulers had brought the ancient throne into disrepute. Greeks and Romans alike invaded and took possession of the country. In 25 B. C., earthquakes wrought great havoc among the ancient temples. Upon the advent of Christianity, followed the destruction of pagan statues and the disfigurement of important inscriptions. Naturally, nothing was done to preserve the temples. Churches were erected within their walls. People that had lost all reverence for the ancient gods lived within the gates of the once sacred enclosures.

The great population of the ancient city has long since passed away. Small villages of mud-dried bricks have supplanted the magnificent city of old. For a long time the ruins of these Theban temples were forgotten, to become revealed to modern civilization in the latter part of the eighteenth century, when the published accounts of French explorations disclosed to the astonished eyes of modern Europe the glories of the great city of the kings.

The plan of modern Thebes gives a very good idea of the position of the buildings of the ancient city. The ruins of the great temples of Luxor

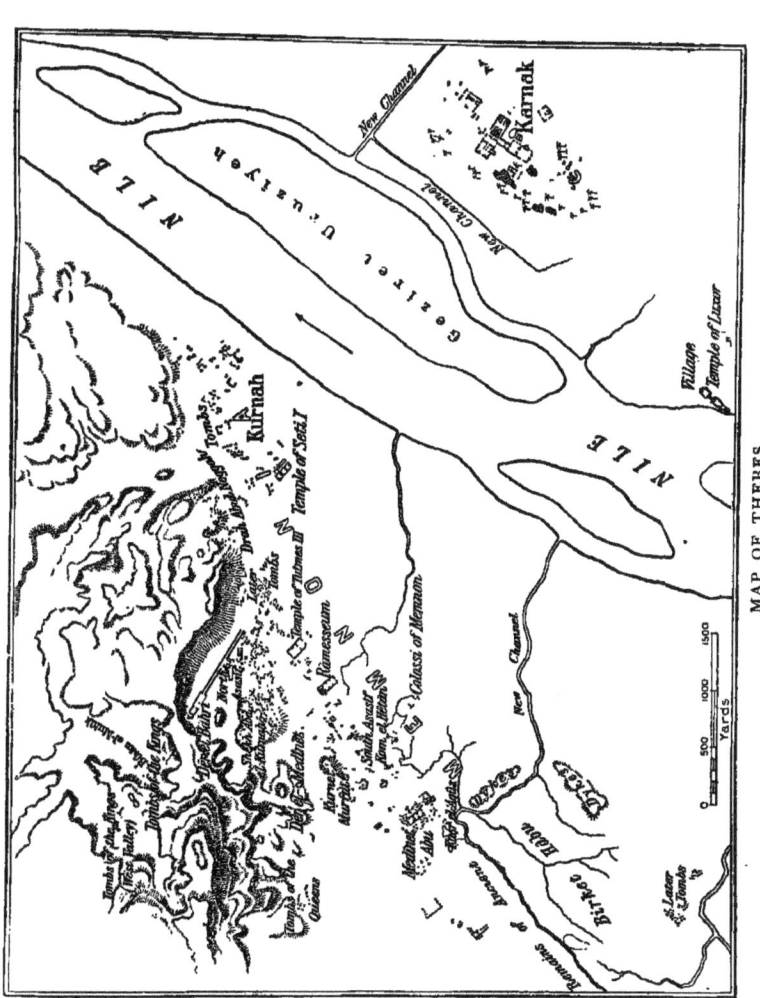

MAP OF THEBES

TEMPLE RUINS: KARNAK

and Karnak are on the east side of the river, and beyond them were the streets of the ancient capital. "Hundred-gated Thebes" as sung by Homer and echoed in the writings of Strabo, Pliny, and Diodorus, has reference to the pylons of these temples. On the west bank was the great necropolis with its vaults cut from the solid rock, its mortuary chapels, and the dwellings of the priests.

The ruins of this mighty period lend their peculiar charm to the landscape, where, within the mountain-girt basin, a valley of never-ceasing fertility, nature revels in perpetual youth. Though the monuments of countless ages speak to us of death, yet life is omnipresent in the verdant crops and graceful palms. Day after day "in his golden boat" the sun sails proudly across the clear blue sky, flooding the valley with rich color and lighting up the sombre faces of the mountains of the desert with iridescent tones.

More than thirty centuries divide the historic past from the life of to-day, yet man's handiwork is seen through them all. Delicate are the carvings, brilliant is the coloring of ornament; wondrous are the cuttings of the hieroglyphic language, which tell us how man has lived, worshipped, and loved, and how the web of life has been woven during this long period of time.

The temple of Luxor is close to the river and during the inundation its columns are washed by the overflowing waters. It is built in several sections, showing that its construction was gradual and under the direction of different kings. The axis of the most northerly section is made to deviate somewhat from that of the main temple. Possibly this was done that the pylons might be more nearly parallel to one of the temples of the Karnak group, as well as to allow for the construction of a direct avenue of sphinxes between the two temples.

In front of the main pylon were two obelisks, and on both sides of the doorway, and between the columns at the end of the first court, stood colossal statues fully forty feet in height. In numerous inscriptions upon the walls, Rameses II. claims for himself the chief glory connected with the construction of the temple. He also relates his wondrous triumphs in the affairs of

TEMPLE OF LUXOR FROM THE RIVER

TEMPLE OF LUXOR: PYLON AND OBELISK

war. On the left wall of the main pylon is seen the king in his chariot drawn by spirited horses, while on the right he is represented in his camp, surrounded by his officers.

The poem of Pentaur also is inscribed upon the temple. The poet recounts how the king, Rameses II., when deserted by his warriors, called upon the god Ammon-Ra for aid, reminding him of the great deeds he had done in his name and of the temples he had erected in his honor. As the story runs, the foe was vanquished, although the king, unaided save by the god, faced twenty-five hundred chariots of war. "I beseech thee. O father Ammon, look upon me here in the midst of countless foes that are strange to me. All nations have united themselves against me and I am alone and no one is with me." The entire description as given in the translation is intensely interesting. Though the king claims superhuman power through divine aid, his story is not more marvellous than those that have come down to us through other avenues of historic tradition.

About a mile and a half from Luxor and a

78 THE LAND OF THE TEMPLE BUILDERS.

short distance from the river are the great ruins of Karnak. Not one temple but many temples, not one pylon but many pylons, mark the site of monuments the very ruins of which are the grandest in the world. Like stanch soldiers, these half-buried pylons rear their prodigious forms as if triumphant over Time, the destroyer of material things.

One travels across the fields along an embankment of earth until he reaches the ancient processional roadway, which, though in ruins to-day, is still beautiful with its arching palm-trees and its mutilated fragments of sculptured sphinxes. Down this avenue in the late afternoon when the palms spread their shadows across the path, one may approach the magnificent pylon of Khonsu. Here again one seems to be treading holy ground and to be intruding within these temples of the gods once so sacred to the pagan heart; although constructed more than thirty centuries ago, despoiled by the hand of man and shattered by earthquakes and disturbing elements, still the force of their religious purpose impresses the beholder with wonderful solemnity.

INTERIOR OF THE TEMPLE OF LUXOR

TEMPLE OF KHONSU: KARNAK

The temple of Khonsu is the one usually seen in illustrations and is often spoken of as "the temple of Karnak." Although of large proportions, it is small in comparison with the great temple that lies to the northeast.

A short distance in front of Khonsu is the ornamental gateway, noble in size and conception. Across its entablature is stretched a beautifully-carved representation of the winged disk, the emblem of divine protective power. The wall-surface of this pylon is covered with inscriptions, and with pictures of the kings paying tribute to their gods. The temple is of fine proportions and wonderfully preserved. Little light penetrates the darkened chambers, sufficient only to render discernible the fantastic outlines of innumerable inscriptions. Here one seems to breathe the very atmosphere of a remote age ahd to touch the link that binds the present with the dim past.

The temple was erected by Rameses III., in honor of Khonsu, the Theban god, who was supposed to represent the youthful Ammon. In an inscription found on a papyrus roll, Rameses is represented as saying: " I built a house in Thebes for thy son Khonsu, of good hewn stone, its doors covered with gold adorned with electrum like the celestial horizon."

Leaving this temple and passing toward the north, one reaches the first main pylon of Karnak — the great temple of Ammon. This immense portal — three hundred and seventy-two feet wide, one hundred and forty-two feet high, and sixteen feet thick — faces the Nile. The remains of an avenue of sphinxes stretch from the temple toward the river. In imagination we go back to the time of ancient pageantries, when the king and priests and devout men paid tribute to their gods. We picture the gayety of the scene: the state barges, with decorations in gold and brilliant color, sailing slowly up the Nile greeted by choirs upon the river bank singing praise-songs to the great Ammon. We can see the boats draw up one by one at the landing-place, from them passing priests and dignitaries, whose jeweled gowns sparkle in the bright sun. Finally the procession, led by the king and the high priest, is formed. Slowly it wends its way

GREAT PYLON — TEMPLE OF AMMON : KARNAK

FIRST COURT—TEMPLE OF AMMON: KARNAK

toward the temple, spreading itself like a gay oriental carpet at the feet of the couchant sphinxes, while above the pylon float the colors of Upper and Lower Egypt.

Within the first court of the temple gather the sacred hosts. Toward the sanctuary the procession moves slowly and with rhythmic step. Gradually it decreases in numbers as the inner chambers are reached, until finally the king and the high priest enter the "holy of holies"; in the outer chambers remain the elect few whose various offices entitle them to admission within the sacred walls.

The first great peristyle court, measuring three hundred and thirty-eight feet in width by two hundred and seventy-five feet in depth, accommodated a large number of people. The great pylon formed its portal; while at the other end of the court a second pylon with double doorway framed the entrance to that wonderful Hall of Columns, the marvel of ages.

This hall measures three hundred and thirty-eight feet in width and one hundred and seventy feet in depth. The broad central passageway is formed by a double row of columns measuring seventy feet in height. The shafts of the columns are nearly twelve feet in diameter and thirty-six feet in circumference. The capitals are eleven feet in height, and their enormous corolla-shaped tops spread out as though to support the very dome of heaven. On both sides of the nave are other columns, one hundred and twenty-two in number, each being over forty feet in height and twenty-seven feet in circumference. These columns have bud-shaped capitals supporting a roof lower than that of the nave.

Who can describe this forest of columns, their prodigious size and the power displayed in their construction? Their shafts still reveal elaborate chronicles of the deeds of men of princely power, whose names have long been strange to human lips. Why built they on a scale so vast? Was it to fulfil their conceptions of a spiritual life? Was it with the idea that these monuments should exceed things temporal? Was it to show the triumphant power of the kings that reigned over Upper and Lower Egypt? Or, was it to show the power of their faith in the gods and to per-

GREAT HALL OF COLUMNS — TEMPLE OF AMMON: KARNAK

HYPOSTYLE HALL — TEMPLE OF AMMON: KARNAK

petuate their doctrines of immortality? To us they tell a story of endless labor, of bondage, of kingly ambition, of human sacrifice, of the finite mind endeavoring to reach out blindly to the godhead of its faith. The vastness of their dimensions renders us speechless; we are appalled at their majestic dignity.

The mystery of worship that caused the erection of these temples still pervades the pillared halls. The great stones seem cemented with the life-blood of a bonded people, who, though unknown to the world, have left the imprints of human life upon these colossal time-defying monuments. The sinking sun sends its last rays through the long avenue of columns, forming gigantic shadows that stretch toward the east; while the illumined shafts and capitals reflect the colored decorations that long ago emblazoned their surfaces.

But there remain other parts of this interesting temple to be seen before the god of light shall leave the upper world in darkness. Broken columns, capitals, and obelisks obstruct the way leading to the sanctuary. Two well-preserved obelisks still remain on their pedestals. One, seventy-six feet in height, was erected by Thothmes I., and inscriptions upon the shaft bear record of this great king, who is compared to the god Horus. The second obelisk of red granite was erected by Queen Hatasu. It is nearly one hundred feet in height. A part of one inscription reads: " Hatasu erected this as a monument to her father, Ammon, the lord of the throne of both lands." This beautiful shaft, with its crown and decorations of gold glistening in the sun, was easily to be seen from every part of the ancient city and was reverenced as a royal tribute to a great divinity.

Upon reaching the sanctuary, we find that it is divided into two parts, one compartment facing to the west and one to the east; the latter being constructed by Thothmes III., who, desiring to build additions to the temple, conceived the idea of extending the plan toward the east. The granite sanctuary is the oldest part of the structure, as is true of the sanctuaries of all other Egyptian temples. The decorations that appear upon the walls and pylons leading to the sacred chamber indicate inversely the different periods

GRANITE SANCTUARY: KARNAK

WALL DECORATION: KARNAK

of decorative art, the earliest being in and about the sanctuary, the later appearing in the chambers and halls in front, which are of more recent construction.

The walls of this enormous temple of Karnak are covered with important inscriptions, which throw much light upon the history of the Egyptians. They are replete with information regarding the exploits of the great king Seti I. and his victories over the enemy. One inscription records in detail various battles, as well as an international treaty between the people of Asia Minor and of Egypt. This treaty of peace between Rameses II. and the prince of Kheta is so complete in its composition and essential points that it is not very unlike the international agreements enacted at the present day.

Extensive ruins of other temples and pylons are scattered over a wide area surrounding the great temple of Ammon. At right angles to the first court and penetrating its side wall, is a temple built by Rameses III., which, although large in dimensions, seems comparatively small in contrast to the great temple of which it is a part. Enormous pylon gateways and an avenue of sphinxes form a processional way from the middle court to the temple of Mut. South of the temple of Ammon is the sacred lake common to every temple. Upon its surface are said to have floated the golden boats of the god.

The ruins should not be visited in the middle of the day, but, rather, when the slanting rays of the afternoon sun heighten the color values, and the long shadows increase the beauty of effect. The most enchanting impression, however, is produced by moonlight. Then the gigantic ruins appear exaggerated in proportions and seem under the spell of some mysterious power. Their enormous columns, like great towers, seem to penetrate the sky. All is quiet in the deserted chambers. Standing within the eternal shadows of the past, one dares not break the silence and is riveted to the ground as if by magic power. How insignificant seems man in the presence of these colossal monuments! How superhuman must have been the strength of the giant builders of the XIXth Dynasty! Yet were these "temples built with hands"!

TEMPLE OF AMMON AND SACRED LAKE, KARNAK

ASSUAN

VIII.

ASSUAN AND PHILÆ.

THE ancient name of Assuan was *Sun ;* meaning an opening or entrance. That is, the city was the gateway to the country beyond the first cataract. The present city of Assuan, five hundred and eighty miles by river from Cairo, is situated at the first cataract of the Nile, and it is the terminus for the caravan road that crosses the desert. Here are loaded upon the merchant boats ivory, india rubber, ostrich feathers, fruit, and other merchandise from the south, to be shipped northward to Cairo and elsewhere.

Opposite Assuan, just below the rapids, is the island of Elephantine, a place esteemed sacred by the ancient Egyptians. The whirling waters of the cataract were supposed to have some mysterious connection with the Nile source, a knowledge of which the priests taught would be revealed to the soul in after-life. By some it was thought that the god of the Nile had his abode in the rapids, and temples erected in his honor formerly stood upon the island, but they have been entirely destroyed. There still remains, however, a well-preserved nilometer of solid masonry, the construction of which was described by Strabo. The nilometer was used for measuring the height of the waters at the time of the overflow of the Nile.

At the left of the roadway, and a short distance south of Assuan, are situated the ancient quarries that have supplied granite for the columns, obelisks, and statues, from the earliest history of Egyptian art. Heaps of stone give evidence of the industry of the great builders.

An obelisk still lies in its native bed. It is ninety-two feet in length, and three sides have been carefully cut, but for some unknown reason it was never separated entirely from the solid rock. The method of separation probably consisted of drilling holes in the rock and filling them with wooden wedges that were afterward saturated with water, the swelling of the wood causing the stone to split.

A part of a pictorial inscription on fragments

THE DESERT HIGHWAY: ASSUAN

OBELISK IN QUARRY: ASSUAN

of stone from the temple of Der-el-Bahri illustrates the manner in which obelisks and colossal statues were transferred from the quarries to the place of erection. In the illustration, two obelisks are loaded upon a large flat-boat or raft. This boat, towed by three parallel groups of ten boats each and connected with them by cable, is followed• by boats of superior build, which were probably used by officers of high rank, judging from the royal emblems with which they are decorated. The leading boats contain soldiers, and pilots that take measurements of the depth of the water in much the same way as do the pilots of to-day. The bow of each boat is fastened to the mast of the preceding boat, that the stern may be free for steering. Each craft carries thirty-two oarsmen, in addition to the officers and other members of the crew, which indicates that fully one thousand men must have been employed to transport these two colossal shafts. The obelisk being a monument of much religious significance, three boats follow the raft, containing priests, who offer frankincense and perform other religious duties.

Some writers believe that the obelisks were landed upon the river-bank opposite the temple and then hauled overland to the place of erection. But, inasmuch as the soil is alluvial, entirely free from stone, and easily moved, it seems reasonable to suppose that the Egyptians, who had the skill to cut such monuments from the quarries, would be equally competent to dig canals from the river to the temple site, and thus convey upon rafts the stones, obelisks, and statues to be used in temple construction. Upon the completion of the building, the canals could be easily filled with earth.

In one of the tombs at Beni-Hassan, however, is a picture representing the process of moving a great statue upon land. The statue is loaded upon a huge sled drawn by a large force of workmen. One man is engaged in pouring water upon the runners to prevent friction; while another stands at the left of the statue and beats time, that the men may work in unison; overseers provided with whips urge the laborers to their task.

Beyond the quarries and six miles from Assuan

RIVER NILE: PHILÆ IN DISTANCE

ISLAND OF PHILÆ

is the island of Philæ. It may be reached by several routes, the most popular being that desert road which is the highway to Abyssinia and the Soudan, and which is fully described by the ancient Greek geographer. This road consists of a wide path through the sands, and is bounded in many places by a rock formation, dark in color, conical in shape, and often resembling small towers. A more interesting approach to Philæ is by the path along the river-bank. The first part of the journey is made by the desert highway, when a sharp turn to the right through drifting sands brings one to the water's edge; thence the path leads among cone-shaped rocks, past the rapids, to a point opposite the island.

A visit to Philæ by this route is not soon forgotten. As the beautiful island comes into view one greets it with the delight of having found a truly familiar landscape, so frequently has it been photographed and reproduced for one's pleasure. Situated in a sharp bend of the river and surrounded by the purple mountains of the desert, this picturesque island, with its graceful palm-trees and its well-preserved temples, presents a picture of surpassing beauty.

The island of Philæ is about thirteen hundred feet long and five hundred feet wide. According to legend, here was one of the graves of Osiris, and this belief made it a place of pilgrimage for the Egyptians. It was not, however, held in reverence by Egyptian worshippers alone; as the principal temple was sacred to Isis, many Greek and Roman pilgrims also visited the island. The landing-stage of ancient times was situated at the south end of the island, in order to avoid the rocks and currents of the north side. Here the boats of worshippers approached in ceremonial procession.

The temple of Isis is built in different sections and shows much irregularity of plan. The worshippers first entered a small forecourt bounded by columns connected by stone balustrades several feet in height. Upon one of the columns is inscribed: " The good god lord of both worlds, Ra-kheper-ka, son of the sun, and lord of the diadems, Nectanebus, the ever-living, erected this sumptuous building for his mother Isis, the be-

TEMPLES OF PHILÆ

HYPOSTYLE HALL—TEMPLE OF ISIS. PHILÆ

stower of life, in order to enlarge her dwelling with excellent work, for time and for eternity."

From this small forecourt, the worshipper entered a large court, or area, of irregular shape; this was much wider at one end than at the other, and bounded on both sides by a covered colonnade. These colonnades are of great beauty, the capitals presenting much variety of design. The east colonnade still shows traces of color applied to the carved surface. The pictorial inscriptions on the great entrance pylon bear evidence of the destructive hand of the Coptic iconoclast, who felt it his duty to chisel away representations of the pagan gods. Beyond the pylon is another court, bounded on one side by several chambers and on the opposite side by a small temple. Passing through the second pylon, which forms the façade to the main temple, one stands within a hypostyle hall, the roof of which is supported by ten columns. The color upon the capitals is so remarkably preserved that it is hard to realize it was applied twenty centuries ago. The principal colors used are green, blue, and dark and light red. It is evident that the decorators did not feel bound to imitate the colors of nature in the foliage sculptured upon the stone. They conventionalized the decoration to the extent of employing color sometimes in direct contrast to nature. Upon the ceiling of the hall are painted the astronomical representations so common in the decoration of all temples. Some of the small buildings outside the temple also contain remarkable pictorial decorations, the most famous being that of the Nile source, one of the few attempts at landscape drawing found upon Egyptian monuments.

The Kiosk, frequently known as "Pharaoh's bed," is a small temple or pavilion, probably constructed in the first century A. D., and showing Greek influence. While its proportions are somewhat faulty, yet, contrasted with other temples of Philæ, it is the most beautiful upon this holy island of the Egyptians.

Unfortunately, these temples are directly affected by the great dam built across the Nile. Already the waters cover the island and half submerge the temples. In a short time these buildings that have survived over two thousand years will be destroyed.

PHILÆ: THE KIOSK

DENDERAH: PYLON AND TEMPLE.

IX.

THE TEMPLES OF DENDERAH, ESNEH, AND KOM OMBO.

THUS far the temples have been selected and described without regard to relative situation or time of building. The temple of Edfu was given first attention because it is one of the best-preserved structures in Egypt. The Karnak group, which comprises the largest edifices, next received consideration, while the picturesque environment of the island of Philæ, with a description of its interesting temples, naturally followed. Many other temples are scattered along the banks of the Nile, some having been excavated in their entirety and others only in part. There are memorial chapels, too, on the west bank at Thebes, opposite Karnak, but these will be described in connection with the great tomb-fields or city of the dead, of which they form a part. Three other temples, however, deserve mention here, the temples at Denderah, Esneh, and Kom Ombo; while a fourth, that at Abydos, is described under the subject of "Sculpture," because of its beautiful relief decorations.

Although four hundred miles from Cairo, the temple of Denderah is one of the first to be visited by the tourist in ascending the Nile. This temple is some distance from the river and is approached through fields of growing grain. In the distance the Libyan mountains rise, their precipitous cliffs sparkling in the afternoon sun. A great mound — the accumulation of countless ages — looms into view, completely surrounding the temple and reaching to the level of its roof. Excavators have removed the *débris* in and about the building; but, to reach the floor, it is necessary to descend a long flight of steps.

The temple was dedicated to Hathor, the Egyptian Venus. Each of the columns that support the first great hall bears on the four faces of its capital the head of this goddess with the cow's horns, surmounted by the sculptured relief of a house, symbolic of Hathor and of the birth-house of Horus. The inscriptions show that much of

DENDERAH : MOUND OF ANCIENT CITY

TEMPLE OF DENDERAH. HYPOSTYLE HALL

the present temple was built during the reigns of the last of the Ptolemies and the first of the Roman emperors; but the decorations and the quality of the sculptures in the crypts indicate that the original foundations of the temple date back to the rule of the early Egyptian kings.

Upon the ceiling of the first hall are two immense drawings of the goddess Nut, symbolizing the vault of heaven. She is represented as a very tall woman bending forward, with the tips of her fingers touching the earth. The central part of the ceiling between the columns is decorated with a series of winged forms, gray in color and set in panels of a blue ground bordered with stars. The decorations upon the walls and columns illustrate various ceremonies performed by the king in the presence of the goddess. On both sides of the passageway, beyond the first great hall and around the sanctuary, are numerous small chambers. In these, preparations were made for the religious fêtes. One was used as a laboratory where were prepared the oils and perfumes; another held the vestments of the gods and the consecrated material relating to the ceremonies; another served as the treasury; while others contained the offerings of Upper and Lower Egypt. Each room was adapted to some religious purpose. Upon the walls of the two stairways leading to the roof are pictured ceremonial processions; these, in their composition, are somewhat suggestive of the Parthenon frieze. The figure of Isis, crowned with the emblematic horns of the cow and with the disk, constantly recurs, while sacrificial scenes, and figures carrying sacred emblems, are often repeated.

Beneath the foundation walls of the temple are long narrow passageways or crypts, about three feet wide and approached by stone steps. Bats cling to the walls in countless numbers and the atmosphere seems to have been imprisoned for ages. In these secret corridors were probably hidden the gold and silver statues of the divinities, but it is not possible to determine the full purpose of their construction. They are beautifully decorated and wonderfully preserved, the color in many instances still remaining on the relief figures. The work of the artist is done

SMALL TEMPLE: DENDERAH

TEMPLE OF ESNEH

with great accuracy of detail; figure, head-dress, and clothing standing out in exquisite relief.

A high projecting wall extends around the temple roof, in one corner of which is a small chapel. Outside the temple of Hathor are smaller temples partially excavated, and pylons appear here and there among the ruins of the great city, probably gateways to temples of which nothing remains but heaps of broken stones and piles of dust.

Continuing the journey eighty miles above Denderah, and passing the Theban ruins already described, we stop at Esneh to visit the one excavated chamber of its buried temple. Modern Esneh has a population of nine thousand inhabitants and is a place of considerable prosperity. The town has been raised to such a height by the constant accumulations of *débris*, that the streets and houses cover the temple. Only the hypostyle hall, a room one hundred feet long, fifty feet wide, and thirty-five feet high, has been excavated.

To reach the floor of this hall one must descend a long flight of steps. The roof is supported by twenty-four columns of sandstone, each nearly eighteen feet in circumference. The shafts are surmounted by a great variety of capitals, which differ not only in form but also in height, an irregularity that was offset by making the horizontal cuttings or annuli on the same level. The capitals are decorated with ornaments taken from plant forms, beautifully carved in low relief, color having been applied after an almost perfect finish had been secured by the sculptor.

Unlike the temple of Esneh, that of Kom Ombo, lying close to the river upon a high embankment, has been thoroughly excavated, so that its floor and chambers show little trace of its long burial beneath accumulated soil. Care is taken by the government to keep it free from drifting sands.

This magnificent ruin — consisting of a few colossal columns surmounted by fine capitals, fragments of walls, ceilings, and beautiful cornice, together with a few broken shafts — is all that remains of the double temple of the gods. Nevertheless, it presents an imposing

TEMPLE OF KOM OMBO

TEMPLE OF KOM OMBO: WALL DECORATION

appearance from the river below. The present temple was erected in the time of the Ptolemies, but, like nearly all temples of Egypt, the original foundation is of a very early period.

Contrary to the general plan of Egyptian temples, Kom Ombo was dedicated to two triads of gods and had two sanctuaries approached by separate passageways. Dedication scenes, inscriptions relating to festivals and to the worship of gods, and astronomical representations cover the walls in great profusion. Most elaborate and beautiful head-dresses are sculptured in low relief upon the heads of the kings. Over the doorways are exquisitely-carved winged disks, highly colored, while the roof of the central passageway is decorated with the same design on a blue ground. In the doorways are to be seen holes about six inches deep, drilled into the threshold and lintel stones. In these cavities turned the pivots of. the hinges on the great doors that swung open to admit the priests for worship at the sacred altars of the Egyptian gods.

X.
THE TOMBS OF THE ANCIENT EMPIRE.

TOMBS are scattered all along the banks of the Nile. Except at Memphis and a few other places, they are situated far up from the river and cut into the face of the limestone mountains. The two great burial-grounds of the ancient Egyptians are at Sakkarah, west of the site of the city of Memphis in Lower Egypt, and in the mountains west of Thebes in Upper Egypt.

Memphis is much older than Thebes; consequently the tombs and their decorations belong to an earlier period. The religion of the Egyptians underwent a change during the period between 3000 B. C. and 1500 B. C., which naturally affected the character of the decorations illustrating their belief. Within the tombs of Sakkarah one finds decorations that picture the life of men on earth, their possessions, and the

BEDRASHEN NEAR SITE OF ANCIENT MEMPHIS

PYRAMID OF SAKKARAH

things they enjoyed, with little reference to the after-life, except in providing a portrait-statue for the spirit. At Thebes, on the contrary, the inscriptions relate largely to the judgment and to the transmigration of the soul after death.

The great necropolis of Sakkarah stretches along the desert for a distance of nearly five miles, with an average width of one-third of a mile. Within this burial-ground are found rock-cut caves, mastabas, and those great burial-chambers, the pyramids. Everywhere are treacherous openings of unexcavated tombs, while bits of mummy cloth and human bones strew the ground. Thousands and perhaps millions of human beings have been interred in this great cemetery. Innumerable relics have been taken from the tombs to supply museums and private collections of antiquities, yet the supply is far from being exhausted.

Sakkarah is approached by way of the site of the city of Memphis. But little is left of that once-populous city of antiquity, dating back to the reign of the pyramid-builders. Without doubt vast numbers of its buildings were made of sun-dried bricks that have long since crumbled to dust, while the material used in the erection of its temples has been utilized in Cairo and elsewhere in more modern times. Here and there are to be seen foundation stones; but they give no idea of the buildings once standing upon them.

One of the most conspicuous objects found here is the colossal statue of Rameses II. It is of admirable workmanship, of a character similar to those found at Thebes. Upon this very spot may have been erected the temple of Ptah, the statue standing at its portal.

The tombs beyond are of two kinds: the mastaba and the rock chambers. The mastaba is usually built of solid masonry and is rectangular in shape. The exterior surface of its walls slopes inward, somewhat in the form of a very low truncated pyramid. The door or entrance is generally made to face the east, while in the pyramid it is on the north side. In all probability the wealthy class of Egyptians began early in life to plan the construction of tombs corresponding with their rank and station. The tombs

MEMPHIS: COLOSSAL STATUE OF RAMESES II.

STATUE OF TI: CAIRO MUSEUM

were lined with smoothly-cut stone, and decorated by the sculptor in relief and then by the painter in color. The tomb was divided into sections or chambers. The first chamber was the memorial hall or chapel, in which gathered the members of the family to pay respect to the dead and to leave offerings of food for the spirit life. On the west side of the mastaba, toward the setting sun, was the well or shaft leading to the sepulchral vault in which was placed the mummy. In the serdabs, or niches, behind the stone lining of the tomb were placed life-like statues of the occupant. These portrait-statues were carefully hidden from view to prevent destruction.

In this portrait-sculpture, which was at its best three thousand years before Christ, we find an interpretation of the belief that the Egyptians entertained regarding the after-life. Every Egyptian believed that man's being is composed of several distinct parts, of which the most important was the Ka, or double, as it is sometimes called. It represented the personality of the deceased, that mysterious abstraction which was an essential element of his being during life and which survived him after the death of the body. The Ka occupied the tomb, and it was therefore necessary to provide for its entertainment as well as for its sustenance, until the time when it should reunite with the body. In case the body or mummy were destroyed, the statue would take its place. During the separation of the Ka from its body, it led an independent existence. We give food to the body during life, but the moment the spirit departs the body no longer needs nourishment. The Egyptians, however, believed that it was the spirit, the double or Ka, which had been fed in the flesh and that, in its separation from the body, it should still be provided for. Consequently, profuse offerings of food and drink were left in the tomb for the silent occupant.

This thought of providing for the Ka after death was common among the Egyptians for thousands of years, as is shown by the numerous inscriptions and pictures, some of which belong to the early, and some to the more recent, tombs. Bread, beef, geese, wine, beer, and other provisions were furnished. Apparently the Egyp-

TEMPLE OF KOM OMBO: FOOD OFFERINGS

TOMB OF TI: SAKKARAH

tians learned in time to feel that the mere representation of such offerings in some way took the place of the real substance, and pictures of these offerings were made upon the walls of the tombs. Texts written upon the walls invoked all visitors to offer a prayer, or to make a contribution, in behalf of the Ka, which inhabited the tomb with the mummy while the soul was undergoing its journey in the unknown world. The destruction of the Ka meant the total annihilation of the principle of life.

This ancient people believed absolutely in the immortality of the soul; in the resurrection of the body; in the final reunion of the body, soul, and Ka, and of all the elements of the composite nature of man.

One of the best examples of the mastaba with its decorations is the tomb of Ti. Ti was a dignitary of high rank, employed as privy-counsellor to a king of the Vth Dynasty. He was a man of humble parentage, who had risen to a place of high honor, his wife being a member of the royal family.

An inclined passageway leads down to the

opening of the tomb. Passing through a small anterior court upon which are pictured gift-offerings, one enters the main hall, rectangular in shape, its roof being originally supported by twelve piers. Here were performed rites in honor of the departed spirit of Ti. In the centre of the room is the shaft leading to the tomb-chamber below, where lay the sarcophagus. The walls of the chambers of the tomb are covered with pictures and inscriptions arranged in horizontal panels, each about two feet in height and together reaching from the floor to the ceiling. In these panels are wonderfully accurate relief drawings of animals, birds, and the like, and of sacrificial and domestic scenes. The decorations indicate the great prosperity of a wealthy man of the kingdom. Behind the lining of the walls were constructed the serdab niches, in one of which was found the statue of Ti, now preserved in the museum at Cairo.

Through a study of the ancient Egyptians' belief in the immortality of the soul and the consequent preservation of the body after death, we arrive at the true purpose of the construction

TOMB OF TI: WALL DECORATION

PYRAMID OF CHEOPS

of the pyramids situated along the plateau of the great burial-grounds of which the necropolis of Sakkarah is a part.

Even a man of humble origin who had risen to importance might erect, for the reception of his mummy and his portrait-statues, a tomb that should withstand the ages. It behooved a greater man, such as the king of all Egypt, to raise a monument consistent with his rank and power, in the form of a pyramid that should bear testimony to his greatness centuries after he had passed away. And they builded better than they knew, for, when Joseph was sold into Egypt and became ruler over Pharaoh's household, the pyramids west of Cairo had endured for more than a thousand years.

The great pyramid of Cheops, it will be remembered, is seven hundred and fifty feet square at its base and four hundred and fifty feet in height. The entrance was found forty-eight feet above the foundation. The first passageway is four feet in height and a little over three feet in width. It was made to descend a distance of three hundred and twenty feet. This passageway to subterranean vaults was doubtless built in order to lead from the true location of the sarcophagus any who might break into the tomb.

At a distance of sixty feet from the entrance and at a point originally blocked up by huge stones, is the beginning of a long inclined corridor leading to the centre of the pyramid. The first section of this passage is one hundred and twenty-three feet in length, and five and one-half feet in height. A horizontal passageway leads to what is called the "Queen's Chamber," a room eighteen feet square and twenty feet high. The ascending corridor continues for another distance of one hundred and fifty-five feet, and this part is twenty-eight feet in height and of a width varying from three and one-half feet at the lower end to about seven feet at the upper end. At the end of this corridor is another narrow horizontal passage connecting with the "King's Chamber." Nothing was found in this chamber but the remains of a granite sarcophagus.

The "King's Chamber" is thirty-five feet long, seventeen feet wide, and nineteen feet high. The floor is one hundred and forty feet above the

ENTRANCE TO PYRAMID OF CHEOPS

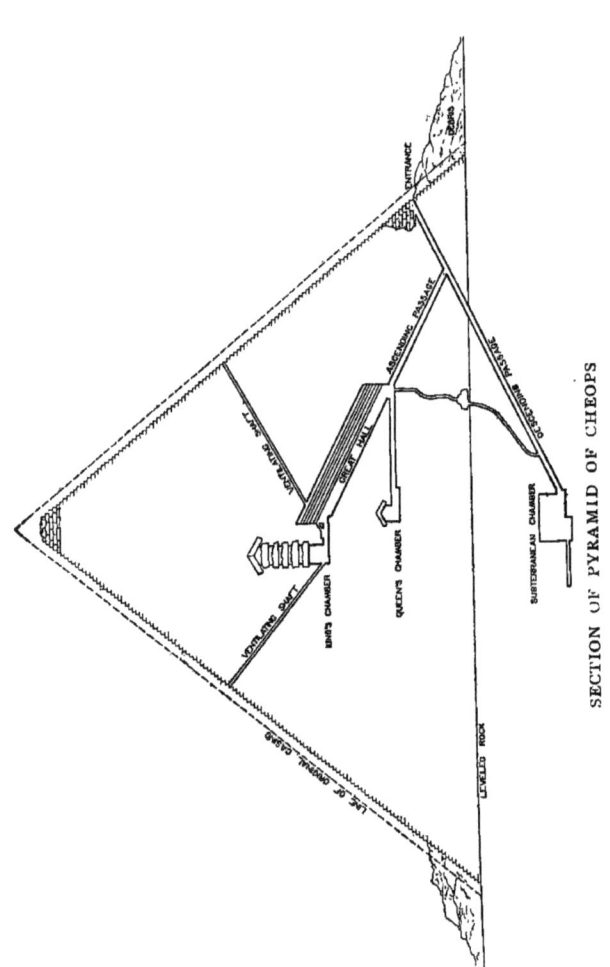

SECTION OF PYRAMID OF CHEOPS

foundation. The walls and ceiling of the room are lined with granite. In order to relieve the pressure, five horizontal slabs, with spaces intervening, were placed above the main roof of the hall. In the last space were found inscriptions in red paint upon the stones, with the name of Khufu (Cheops) upon them. Two small air-shafts were carried obliquely upward to the outside surface of the pyramid; one being nearly two hundred and forty feet in length.

The second pyramid, that of Chephren, although not so large as that of Cheops, contains nearly five million tons of masonry. Its passageways leading into the interior chambers are similar in construction to those in Cheops, but are not so easy of access. The "King's Chamber" is of about the same size as that in the first pyramid. In it was found a sarcophagus that had been ransacked and was filled with *débris*.

In the third pyramid the tomb-chambers are below the foundation, and cut into the solid rock. In one was found a sarcophagus, which, according to the inscription, once contained the body of Mycerinus, its builder. This pyramid is very interesting as furnishing an illustration of the fact, that, even so far back as the time of the pyramid-builders, there was the desire to construct a roof having the appearance of an arch. This was secured in the tomb-chamber by leaning stones one against another at an angle, and cutting away the inner surface so as to produce the appearance of a vault.

As has been said, the remains of sarcophagi found in these pyramids show conclusively the use for which they were constructed, and also illustrate the religious thought regarding the preservation of the body against all possible attempts at annihilation.

One of the chief objects of interest associated with the pyramids is the Sphinx of the desert. Hewn out of the solid rock to a height of sixty-six feet and spreading its great length one hundred and forty feet along the ground, it lies like some huge petrified form of prehistoric birth, half buried in the undulating sands. A tablet that has been found records the fact, that as early as the time of Thothmes III., about 1500 B. C., it was still partly covered with sand; for on

THE SPHINX

TEMPLE OF THE PYRAMIDS

this tablet Thothmes makes record of a dream in which he is entreated by the Sphinx to clear away the sand.

To the Egyptians the Sphinx was a symbol of Horus, the early morning sun, — the new-born light of morning, which had conquered darkness and overcome death with life. Facing the east, the Sphinx reflects the brilliancy of the sunrise, which illuminates the world after its conflict with the powers of darkness. It was thought that the kings were elected to represent the sun-god upon the earth, and the Sphinx was therefore symbolic of the divine nature of their mission.

Near the great Sphinx is a granite temple, or tomb, discovered in 1853. Inscriptions indicate that this temple, which lies below the level of the sand, was constructed by the pyramid-builders. The blocks of granite and alabaster that line the various chambers, and the granite piers that support the roof of the largest chamber, still have a most beautiful lustre. In a deep well in a corner of one of the rooms were found nine statues of Chephren.

Numerous other tombs of great interest have been discovered near the pyramids, and undoubtedly great numbers still remain to be excavated, as the drifting sands shall disclose their sites.

Before leaving the necropolis of Sakkarah, one should visit the tombs of the sacred Apis bulls, discovered in 1851 by Mariette Bey, who had been sent to Egypt by the French Government to make an inventory of old manuscripts. While at Cairo, he noticed a number of sphinxes, which he concluded must have been taken from some avenue near by; and, at Sakkarah, he discovered the head of a similar sphinx projecting from the sand. The passage from Strabo describing the Serapeum of Apis came to his mind, and, believing that the sphinx marked the approach to the long-lost tombs and the site of the ancient temple, he immediately gathered workmen and commenced excavations, soon finding that his supposition was correct.

To the ancient Egyptians, the principle that renewed life was represented by the sacred bull, Apis, the living symbol of Osiris. The temple or palace occupied by Apis during life is known

APIS TOMBS: SAKKARAH

SARCOPHAGUS—APIS TOMBS: SAKKARAH

as the Apeum; and the place of his burial, as the Serapeum.

Little remains of the temple; but leading from it is an inclined passage opening into galleries, which, in combined length, are equal to eleven hundred and fifty feet, one gallery alone measuring six hundred and forty feet. Twenty-four granite sarcophagi were found in recessed chambers. These sarcophagi are thirteen feet long, eleven feet high, and nearly eight feet wide, each weighing about sixty-five tons. At least five hundred votive tablets were found in the tomb. Innumerable images of gods, also, and other relics valuable to the Egyptologist, were discovered about the temple site.

Mariette Bey's description of the discovery of these tombs is of extreme interest. He states: "I confess that when I penetrated for the first time, on November 12, 1851, into the Apis vaults, I was so profoundly struck with astonishment that the feeling is still fresh in my mind, although five years have elapsed since then. Owing to some chance which is difficult to account for, a chamber which had been

154 THE LAND OF THE TEMPLE BUILDERS.

walled up in the thirtieth year of the reign of Rameses II. had escaped the notice of the plunderers of the vaults, and I was so fortunate as to find it untouched.

"Although thirty-seven hundred years had elapsed since it was closed, everything in the tomb seemed to be precisely in its original condition. The finger-marks of the Egyptian who inserted the last stone in the wall built to conceal the doorway were still recognizable on the lime. There were also the marks of naked feet imprinted on the sand which lay in one corner of the tomb-chamber. Everything was in its original position, even the embalmed remains of the bull had lain undisturbed for over thirty centuries. Many travellers would think it terrible to live here alone in the desert for a number of years; but such discoveries as that of this tomb produce impressions compared with which everything else sinks into insignificance, and which one constantly desires to renew."

Although of a later period than the tombs of Sakkarah, about 2500 B. C., the inscriptions and

TOMBS OF BENI-HASSAN

EXTERIOR OF TOMB: BENI-HASSAN

THE TOMBS OF THE ANCIENT EMPIRE. 157

decorations in the tombs of the necropolis of Beni-Hassan, one hundred and sixty-two miles from Cairo, also relate to the home life of the Egyptians. The principal tombs, about one-third the way up the side of the barren mountains east of the river and cut into the face of the rock, are similar in principle of construction to those of Sakkarah. In the main chamber, with its roof supported by columns, gathered the relatives to make offerings to the deceased. A shaft, carefully hidden at the time of the burial, leads to the vault where the mummy was deposited in its sarcophagus. The tombs of Beni-Hassan, unlike those of Sakkarah, show little thought and attention given to portrait-sculpture; instead, many small images, known as shabti or respondents, were buried with the mummy.

As at Sakkarah, the decorations of the tomb represent the deceased in his home or engaged in pastimes that interested him during life. Pictures of battles, hunting-scenes, and athletic sports cover the walls. Much of the decoration is painted upon stucco, a process commonly used in many other tombs in Egypt. In some of the inscriptions, the occupant of the tomb sings of his own goodly deeds. Thus, a prince of the XIIth Dynasty seeks to immortalize in stone his benevolent actions toward his fellowmen: "There is no minor that I have put to grief; no laborer that I have turned off; no shepherd that I have imprisoned; no chief of office from whom I have taken his men for forced labor. There were no hungry or miserable in my day, for if a season of want came, I had cultivated all the arable land of the nome of Meh. None hungered; I gave to the widow; I made no distinction between great and small in all that I gave."

INTERIOR OF TOMB: BENI-ḤASSAN

LUXOR

XI.

THE NECROPOLIS OF THEBES.

WE now return to Thebes, two hundred and eighty miles above Beni-Hassan. The great temples erected in honor of the gods, on the east side of the Nile where the ancient city also was situated, have already been described in detail. On the opposite bank of the river are the great necropolis and the remains of its memorial temples. This necropolis may well be called a city of the dead. Many are the tombs cut into the faces of the great cliffs; everywhere is evidence that thousands and tens of thousands of Egyptians found this their last resting-place.

In the ordinary mastaba at Memphis, the memorial chamber formed a part of the tomb-structure. The great kings that erected the pyramids as their sepulchres, however, built memorial temples outside the pyramids, as the ruins of the beautiful temple of the Sphinx testify. In the time of the New Empire, memnonia, temples considerably removed from the tombs, were built at Thebes to commemorate the lives of the rulers. These memorial temples were on the edge of the necropolis that reaches from the border of the desert back to the cliffs, which at this point rise to a great height. These temples not only were used in making sacrifice to the gods and kings, but were, it was believed, places of the actual residence of the double or Ka after death. They were also devoted to ancestor worship.

Although the city proper was located on the east side of the river, there is no doubt that many of its institutions were established in connection with the memorial chapels. There were libraries, houses for the priests, medical schools, embalmers' establishments, and buildings in which to keep the sacred animals. Houses must have been provided for the people employed about the temples. Soldiers probably guarded the sacred buildings. There must have been shops also for the sale of gift-offerings for the dead, and of other articles. Here were to be

DAHABIYEH ON THE NILE OPPOSITE LUXOR

OVERFLOW OF NILE: STATUES OF MEMNON

found the sacred lakes across which the mummy was carried when pronounced by the earthly judges as worthy of burial in the tomb of his fathers. When we consider how extensive are the ruins to-day after a lapse of so many centuries, the mind may imagine to a limited extent what must once have been the magnificence of this great burial-place.

From the river the necropolis is reached after one crosses luxuriant fields of grain. The statues of Memnon, two colossal figures that have attracted the attention of nations almost from the dawn of history, tower far above the waving grain, and guard the beautiful valley. Side by side they sit — silent, inscrutable, as if weighted with the responsibility of some dark secret whispered to them in the far-distant past. Each figure rises sixty-five feet above the ground, and, with its pedestal, is estimated to weigh over one thousand tons. The legs from foot to knee measure twenty feet, while the middle finger of each hand is four and a half feet in length. When the Nile is at its highest level, the water rises above the pedestals of these seated figures.

The land has increased much in height since they were first constructed; some estimate the rise to be nearly twenty-five feet.

The Colossi of Memnon are all that remain of a temple erected by Amenhotep III. Just back of them rose a great pylon, or portal, leading to the forecourt of the temple. Many traditions have come down to us regarding the musical sounds that formerly emanated from the northern statue and might be heard soon after sunrise. Following the restoration of this statue by the Roman Emperor, Septimius Severus, the phenomenon ceased.

One cannot but be profoundly impressed as he stands before these figures in the early morning light. Unchangeable as the hills beyond, they seem to look out over the world of man and penetrate the very future with their steadfast gaze. They have seen gay processions move out of the city of Thebes and cross the beautiful plains, advancing in the direction of the sacred burial-grounds; they have been the silent witnesses of festal scenes held in honor of Amenhotep, whose temple they guarded; they

STATUES OF MEMNON

THE RAMESSEUM AND TOMB FIELDS

have beheld empires rise and fall at their feet; they have known of Greek and Roman invasion. They have seen the early Christian deface the pagan temples; and the Mohammedan build his house among the Egyptian monuments, unmindful of their sacred significance. No statues erected by the hands of men seem more truly endowed with the spirit of consciousness. Could they but speak, they might tell the story of the ages: but their secrets they do not divulge.

At no great distance from the statues of Memnon are the ruins of the Ramesseum, Medinet-Abu, Der-el-Medinet, and Der-el-Bahri. The Ramesseum, also known as the Memnonium of Rameses II., is in a fairly good state of preservation. From the inscriptions, we learn that it was erected by Rameses II. and dedicated to the deified shades of his departed ancestors, in gratitude for his rescue from the hands of the Kheta, a people of Asia Minor. The poem of Pentaur, commemorating the rescue, is inscribed upon this temple, as well as upon those of Luxor and Karnak. The colossal statue of Rameses II. stood within the first court. When in position, this enormous granite figure rose to a height of nearly sixty feet. One may well marvel how a statue weighing two million pounds could have been cut from the quarries at Assuan and placed in position upon its pedestal. Though we may devise the means theoretically and assume that canals were dug from the river to the foundations of the temple, so that great stones could be floated to the very point of destination, yet we may still wonder how the statue could have been cut from its rocky bed, placed upon floats, and reared in the court of the temple. It is known that in 60 A. D., at the time Deodorus visited Egypt, this statue stood in place. It was undoubtedly thrown down and mutilated by the Christians after the Edict of Theodosius against pagan worship. Even in its condition to-day, lying in fragments upon the ground, its proportions are astounding.

Unlike the Ramesseum, the temple of Medi- net-Abu was constructed under several rulers and during different epochs. Its ruins, which lie within the mound of an ancient town, have

THE RAMESSEUM: COLOSSAL STATUE OF RAMESES II.

EXCAVATIONS: MEDINET-ABU

THE NECROPOLIS OF THEBES. 173

been recently excavated. Pylons, walls, and columns are in a state of good preservation. The entire structure can readily be divided into three or more distinct sections or temples. There is no doubt that the building was erected as a memorial hall and devoted to ancestor worship. Most interesting inscriptions and decorations, illustrating the procession at the beautiful " Festival of the Staircase," are found upon the walls of the second court of the large temple. This festival was celebrated at the time of the new moon, especially that of the first harvest-month. The course of the moon in the heavens was represented by a series of fourteen steps corresponding to fourteen days; hence the name, " Festival of the Staircase." This festival was one of the great Egyptian celebrations held in honor of Khem (Min), the god of reproductiveness. The new moon, rising in the sky after an absence of many nights, was symbolic of the new life of the soul after its separation from the body.

The decoration representing the various ceremonies connected with this festival, extends around the greater part of two sides of the court walls of the temple. First appears the king, Rameses III., seated upon a throne borne by twelve princes and dignitaries of the kingdom. The throne is decorated with the figures of lions. Attendants, walking by the side of the throne, fan the king, while two winged goddesses of justice, wearing the feather of truth upon their heads, follow his royal presence. The part of the procession preceding and following the king is pictured in two parallel rows, and is composed of musicians, dignitaries, priests, and other members of the royal household. Before the king is stationed his body-guard, each member bearing a shield, spear, and sword. Here the king is represented offering to Khem gifts of bread, beer, cattle, and geese. Rameses III. advances to meet him; above the head of the monarch hovers the vulture of victory. The sacred bull appears in the procession, with horns shaped like the crescent moon and enclosing the disk. Many sacrificial vessels, emblems, and statues of ancestors also are pictured upon the wall. Four geese are

TEMPLE OF MEDINEI-ABU

TEMPLE OF DER-EL-MEDINET

liberated in the presence of Pharaoh, to announce to all parts of the universe the accession of the new king and the celebration in honor of Khem. Images of the predecessors of Rameses III. are borne by priests.

One of the small temples of the Medinet-Abu group, although built at the time of the Theban kings, bears many of the characteristics of a Proto-Doric temple. The sanctuary is an oblong chamber surrounded by columns that are somewhat Doric in character and similar to those at Beni-Hassan and Der-el-Bahri. A comparison of its columns with those of other temples furnishes ample proof that the Doric column originated in Egypt.

The other important ruins of memorial temples are those of Kurnah and Der-el-Medinet. The temple of Kurnah was erected by Seti I., who dedicated a part of it to his father. Not enough of the temple remains to give a true conception of its former splendor, but the sculptured decorations are of the same excellent character as those in the temple of Abydos, also erected by Seti I. The kings following Seti I. placed upon the temples as full and complete inscriptions as those by their predecessors, but they did not pay the same regard to execution. They employed less skilful artists, and decoration declined gradually into mere pictorial expressions of the deeds and triumphs of the kings, without any earnest attempt at artistic effect.

The temple of Der-el-Medinet, erected in the time of the Ptolemies, was dedicated to the goddess Hathor. Later, it was used as a dwelling-place by monks, who, seeing no element of beauty in a pagan house of worship, defaced many of the inscriptions and decorations. Over one of the doorways is a beautiful winged disk, surmounted by a frieze of Hathor heads in elliptical panels. This winged sun-disk, with the heads of the Uræus serpent, is always a symbol of the victory of Horus over Typhon, the triumph of good over evil. Most interesting bell-shaped capitals, decorated with conventional plant forms in low relief, also are found in this temple.

Back of the memorial chapels rise the limestone cliffs. The immediate foreground of sand

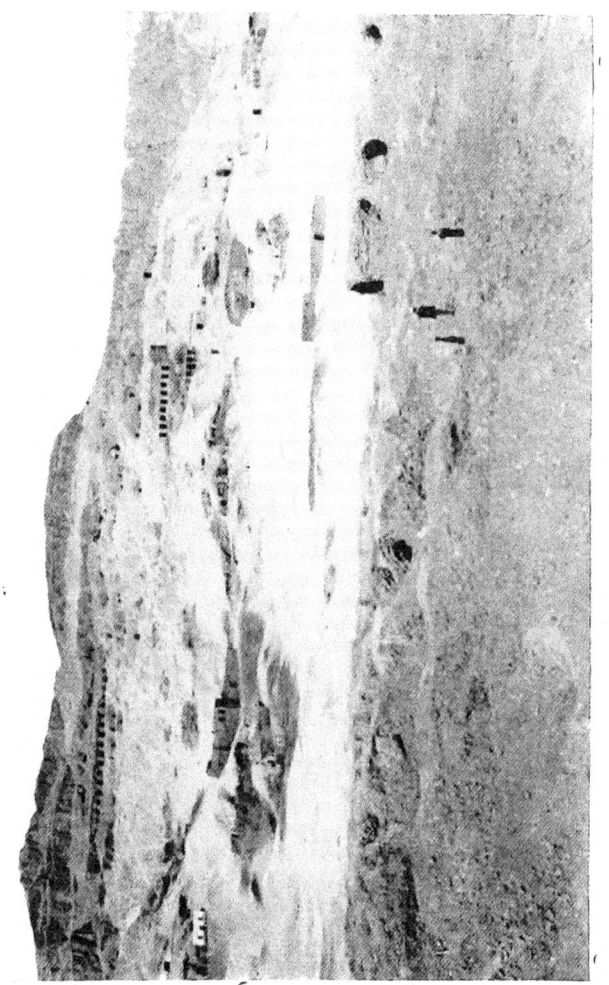

TOMB FIELDS: THEBES

ROAD TO TOMBS OF BIBAN-EL-MULUK

is checkered with the yawning tombs of the great necropolis of the ancient city of Thebes. This burial-ground is divided into sections distinguished by different names. The section most interesting to the traveller is that known as Biban-el-Muluk, which contains the tombs of the kings of the XVIIIth, XIXth, and XXth Dynasties. These tombs are situated in a valley among the mountains, about two miles from the river.

The path leading to the tombs is truly a pathway of the dead. Not a sign of vegetation relieves the eye from the merciless glare of the burning sun. The sand and stones glimmer and vibrate in the intense light and heat. All life seems to have been extinguished under these inexorable rays. It is little wonder that the dry atmosphere should preserve the bodies of the dead for so many centuries.

Between the perpendicular cliffs and along the black rocks and shifting sands, one wends his way slowly to the valley of the tombs of the ancient kings. These tombs are cut in the solid rock; some of them penetrating for a distance of several hundred feet. The descent into a tomb is usually by an inclined plane, but that of Seti I. is entered by a flight of steps. Sometimes a tomb consists of a single passageway terminating in a hall built to receive the sarcophagus. Other tombs, composed of a series of chambers, were intended for the reception of several mummies. When the body had been deposited in its last resting-place, the entrance to its tomb was carefully concealed.

The decorations of these tombs show a very different thought and belief from that of the early tomb-builders. When one enters the tomb-chambers of Biban-el-Muluk, he finds himself in the realm of the dead, not of the living. The occupant is no longer represented with his family, as in the tombs at Sakkarah. His worldly possessions and vocation are no longer pictured upon the walls; domestic scenes, ship-building, and the chase have disappeared. In place of these things of life are pictures of the judgment of the soul and the many trials it is called upon to undergo during the purification process, aided only by such deeds of goodness as the deceased has shown while a dweller among men.

AT THE TOMBS OF THE KINGS: BIBAN-EL-MULUK

ENTRANCE TO A TOMB: BIBAN-EL-MULUK

THE NECROPOLIS OF THEBES. 185

Endless are the uncanny representations of these trials of the soul. Serpents are represented gliding about the rooms or standing erect and darting out their venomous tongues. When placed over the portal, they are supposed to be the guardians of the celestial gates. Hymns of praise are written upon the walls. The gods assume strange forms. But beneath this almost fantastic symbolism lies the comforting thought that, when the soul has finally been weighed and not found wanting, it is rewarded with eternal life. All trials are then at an end. Eternal happiness awaits the soul. The pure spirit may unite with the god and with those who have gone before to dwell in the regions beyond the vault of heaven. The tomb, therefore, is not a permanent residence; it is emblematic of the pilgrimage of the spirit to its heavenly habitation. In successive chambers are pictured the various stages of this purification process, culminating in the assumption of the new and sacred life of the soul.

The most interesting tomb of the Biban-el-Muluk group is that of Seti I., who, it will be remembered, caused to be executed upon the temple of Abydos decorations far superior in beauty of form and line to those of any other period. His tomb also is illustrative of the same artistic treatment. The decorations are very profuse, and are in color. In some instances only the outline of the form appears, showing corrections made by the artist, who never completed his task. Very likely, when the decorations had reached this point, the king died; all work ceased; the body was immediately buried, and the tomb was walled up. This abrupt ending, shown by the unfinished design with the very corrections that the artist purposed to make, gives one the feeling that but a few hours, rather than thousands of years, have elapsed since the worker laid down his brush and colors.

Other tombs are of extreme interest; they were constructed by kings of a later period than that of Seti I. The story of the future life is pictured with as much detail as in the tomb of Seti, but the workmanship is inferior, showing the gradual decline art was beginning to manifest in the Theban Dynasty as early as 1300 B. C.

TOMB OF SETI I : BIBAN-EL-MULUK

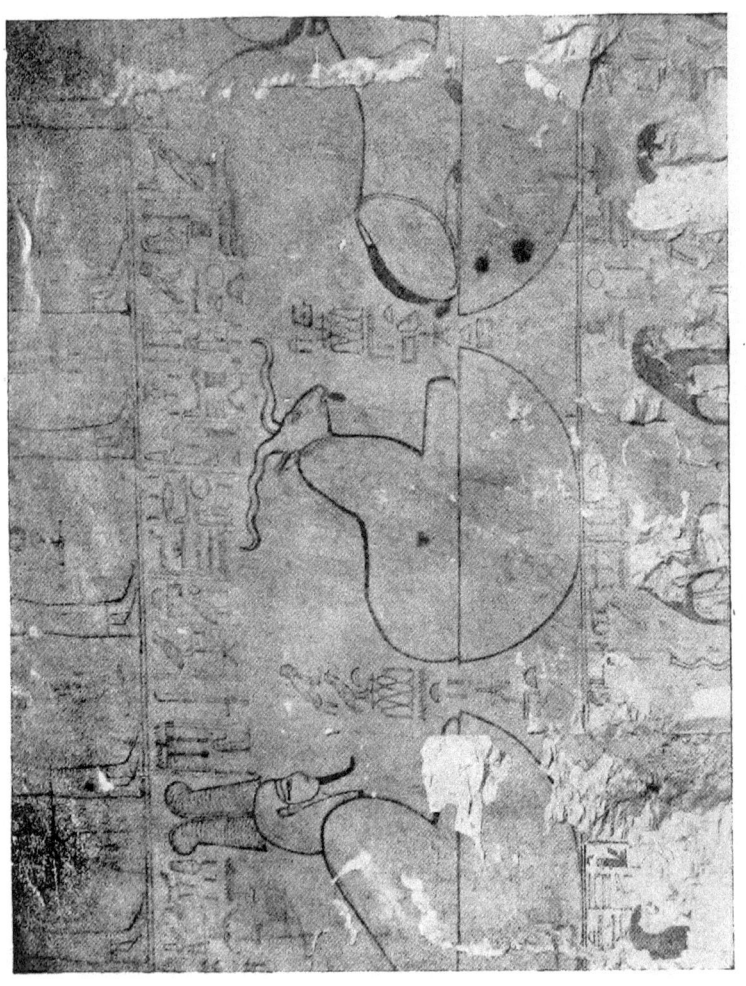

UNFINISHED WALL DECORATION: TOMB OF SETI I.

Before leaving the necropolis of ancient Thebes, one should visit the shaft in which, in 1881, were found so many royal mummies belonging to the period approximately represented by the fifteenth century B. C. For some reason not definitely known, but probably to prevent the despoiling of the bodies of the kings and queens by those who pillaged the tombs and temples at the time of the decline of the Empire, the royal bodies were removed from the tombs originally prepared for them at Biban-el-Muluk and placed in one tomb where they could be easily protected. This tomb is entered by a deep vertical shaft upon the face of a high cliff, a short distance to the northwest of the memorial temples of the necropolis. Owing to the *débris* banked up against the cliff by the disintegration of the soft stone, the shaft remained undiscovered for centuries.

It was July 5th, when Emil Brugsch first entered this shaft and found at a depth of thirty-eight feet a horizontal passageway nearly two hundred feet long, ending in a tomb-chamber. Brugsch thus describes the discovery: —

" Every inch of the subterranean passage was

covered with coffins and antiques of all kinds. My astonishment was so overpowering that I scarcely knew whether I was awake or whether it was only a mocking dream. Resting on a coffin, in order to recover from my intense excitement, I mechanically cast my eyes over the coffin lid, and distinctly saw the name of King Seti I., the father of Rameses II., both belonging to the XIXth Dynasty. A few steps farther on, in a simple wooden coffin, with his hands crossed on his breast, lay Rameses II., the great Sesostris himself. The farther I advanced, the greater was the wealth displayed; here Amenhotep I., there Aahmes, the three Thothmes, Queen Aahmes Nefertari, Queen Aahhotep, all the mummies well-preserved; in all 36 coffins, belonging to the kings and their wives, or to princes and princesses."

Many important tombs have since been found; some of these contained the mummy and tomb furniture. The tomb of Iouiya and Touiyou is of especial interest. Some of the furniture from this tomb is illustrated in the last chapter of this book.

INTERIOR OF THE TOMB OF NAKHT: THEBES

TEMPLE OF MEDAMUT

XII.
EARLY DEVELOPMENT OF THE COLUMN.

WHENCE came the Egyptians? We look at the pyramids, the wonderful tombs, the great temples, the slender shafts of the obelisks, the colossi, the many columns, the numberless decorations in intaglio, relief, and color, and ask ourselves the question : By whom were these works of art originated and what of the ages through which they developed? Whence came the seed that produced so perfect fruit? Is Egypt the birthplace of architecture, sculpture, and painting, or did men journeying from the East carry into this country of the Nile a knowledge of the arts and sciences which culminated in the great monuments of antiquity? The buildings of Asia have crumbled; but those of Egypt have withstood time for more than fifty centuries. Whether or not the arts originated in Asia we may never know; but true it is that Egyptian art in all its conceptions and details is of a unique character. It is different from that of any other country, except as the art of other countries shows the influence of that of Egypt. The art of the Nile country, as we know it, is entirely local in character — the art of a peculiar people, who, through thousands of years lived upon the banks of the sacred river, protected from encroachments of the enemy on the east and the west by the death-dealing sands of the desert. The wonder is, that the arts should have continued to develop through such æons of time and show only the peculiarities of one people. That the Egyptians have had great influence upon the art of other countries is evident, and as further excavations are made and more careful study is given to the growth and development of architectural forms and details of ornament, the more clearly is the fact proved that some of the forms perfected by the Greeks had their origin more than a thousand years earlier in the narrow border-lands of the Nile.

This is true of the column, which is one of the most important architectural features in temple

THE RAMESSEUM

COLUMNS: TEMPLE OF LUXOR

EARLY DEVELOPMENT OF THE COLUMN. 197

construction. The Egyptians made great use of the column. They did not make much use of the true arch, although very frequently they curved the roof to imitate the vault of heaven, studding its blue surface with the golden stars of night. In the primitive form of temple construction we must first call to mind a small sanctuary with lintels or roofing-stones carried across from wall to wall and needing no interior support. The time came, however, when more extensive chambers were built. Owing to their size, the horizontal lintel of stone could not be made to reach from wall to wall. It therefore became necessary to support these masses of stone by intermediate piers, which at first were rectangular and without beauty of form and proportion. The clumsy effect of the rectangular pier soon became apparent to the architect and, through a slow process of growth, the column was developed. At first the angles of the pier were cut off, making it octagonal in shape. In time, the pier became many-sided, and, to improve its general appearance, the flat surfaces between the angles were slightly grooved or fluted. Fluted columns dating back twenty-five hundred years before Christ have long been known to exist at Beni-Hassan. They are often called Proto-Doric because they resemble the Greek Doric, although in the Egyptian form there is no capital.

Until lately, it has been held by some writers, that these columns, found in a tomb on the side of the mountains some distance from the river, could not have been known to the Greeks; or, if known, could not have influenced them in the development of the Doric column. Excavations, however, show that similar columns were used elsewhere in Egypt. At Medinet-Abu there is a little temple, constructed about 1400 B. C., which possesses many of the characteristics of a Greek temple, including octagonal columns. At Assuan and Karnak are similar columns, while recently there has been excavated at Thebes the beautiful temple of Der-el-Bahri, in which are many examples of this style of column, including a colonnade with entablature of beautiful proportions. As this temple was erected many centuries after the tombs of Beni-Hassan were constructed, and yet nearly a thousand years before the column was

TEMPLE OF DER-EL-BAHRI

DER-EL-BAHRI: PROTO-DORIC COLUMNS

perfected by the Greeks, the indications are, that, for a period of at least two thousand years, the Egyptians made use of the polygonal form of column. It is natural to suppose, that in this time the Greeks became cognizant of its form and usage.

Not only at Beni-Hassan are Proto-Doric columns used, but in some of the tombs are architectural features that remind one forcibly of other details of Greek construction. For instance, one tomb has a pointed roof, in the centre of which the original stone is left for a thickness of about two feet, filling the space to the ceiling, as though its triangular form was to support the roof like the pediment of a temple. This triangular form not only is retained, but it is also carried down a distance of two feet below a horizontal line, connecting the angles of the roof where it joins the vertical walls. This primitive entablature, with its triangular pediment-form above, is supported by two columns that are strongly Doric in character. The combination of these features produces much the same effect as the façade of a small Greek temple.

The most striking example of the early Doric column is to be found in the temple of Der-el-Bahri, already mentioned, erected by Thothmes I. and Queen Hatasu. The temple takes its present name from the monastery that was in use in the early days of the Christian period. Unlike other temples, it was built in terraces against the vertical wall of the mountain cliffs. An avenue of sphinxes probably led to the river, at a point opposite the avenue of the temple of Karnak on the east bank. This unique temple, rising in four terraces up the steep side of the mountain, was, for a long time, buried under the sand that had disintegrated from the cliffs above; but it has been recently excavated. The excavations have brought to light a remarkable colonnade of sixteen columns, beside other chambers supported by this Proto-Doric form. The various walls and chambers connected with the temple also reveal most interesting pictorial inscriptions, many of which relate to the expeditions directed by Queen Hatasu to the land of Punt, on the eastern coast of Africa. The inscriptions illustrate the scenes connected with the voyage and the

LOTUS DECORATION: KARNAK

CAPITAL: PHILÆ

return of the boats freighted with fruits, incense, precious woods, ebony, animals, natives, and children, from the wonderful country of the East. The story, told in low relief and color, exhibits much skill in execution. Every detail is rendered with precision of line and accuracy of finish.

While it may be easily understood how the polygonal form of column developed from the square pier, the question may be asked: How came the Egyptians to carve capitals in the form of the lotus bud and flower? It seems quite impossible that, at the very conception of the bell-shaped capital, any people could have evolved capitals in direct imitation of a flower. This close imitation, however, was brought about only after a long process of evolution. It must be remembered that the combination of carving and color is characteristic of Egyptian art. Almost every part of the wall-surface of tomb or temple was covered with inscriptions and pictorial decorations involving nature forms. A people so fond of imitating plant forms in color decorations, naturally, in the earliest times, decorated the square piers with drawings of the sacred lotus-flower. Assuming the flower to be painted on a large scale on each of the four faces of the pier in such a way that it occupied the full width of each face, what would be more natural than carefully to cut away the angles of the pier until there remained a cylindrical shaft resembling the stem and flower that had been painted upon its surface? This cutting away probably underwent a slow development; the pier at first being cut so as to leave the flower form in relief only. There still exist at Karnak two stone piers, showing the lotus form in relief as described. Thus, in course of time, were developed many varieties of bell-shaped capitals, all having the same general form, but decorated with different plants. The bud-shaped capital is suggestive of stability, and we find it was used when necessary to support a heavy roof; while the open-flower, or bell-shaped, capitals were more often employed in colonnades and in halls of lighter construction.

The bell-shaped capitals left the quarries cut merely in the general form they were eventually to assume. When they had been put into place,

CAPITAL: PHILÆ

TEMPLE OF PHILÆ: EAST COLONNADE

the sculptor completed the work, chiselling upon their surface the conventional forms of decoration. Seldom are two capitals alike. The colonnade at Philæ not only comprises a great variety of finished capitals but also includes several which, for some unknown reason, were never touched by the sculptor after they had been put into position. The painter, following the sculptor in his work, was not careful to use the exact colors found in nature; as is seen in the first hypostyle hall in the temple of Isis at Philæ, where the colors used were almost in direct contrast to nature. Yet these colors combined are decorative and harmonious, giving to the natural stone a warmth of treatment that is most pleasing. It seems incredible that color applied so many centuries ago should still retain such brilliancy. The temples of Abydos and Philæ, and the tombs that have been recently excavated, show color that must retain almost its original strength.

XIII.
SCULPTURE.

WE have seen why the Egyptians of the Early Empire constructed the strong mastabas that are found on the necropolis of Memphis, and why the kings built the massive pyramids. It was to provide a place of security for the body until the spirit should return to it. And the far-sighted man who had his tomb built during life took no risk as to the possible destruction of the body. He provided portrait-statues according to his means. These statues were hidden away in the secret chambers of the tomb, to be recognized by the returning spirit as its double, in case the mummy should be destroyed. In the earliest historic times, this belief led to the most perfect portrait-sculpture known in Egyptian art. When the thought regarding the value of the portrait-statue changed and less importance was attached to its significance, then sculpture also

STATUES OF RA-HOTEP AND PRINCESS NEFERT: CAIRO MUSEUM

SHEIK-EL-BELED: CAIRO MUSEUM

changed; and, during the Theban period, it assumed a conventional type.

We go back, then, to the earliest known period to find the best examples of sculpture. No one can stand in the presence of the portrait-statues of Ra-Hotep and the Princess Nefert in the Museum of Cairo without being profoundly impressed. Through a period of over five thousand years, these seated statues, modelled in limestone, have preserved the semblance of a characteristic type of the Egyptians of the Ancient Empire, at the same time illustrating an art of great antiquity. The faces are wonderfully life-like; and the color that is added to the sculpture intensifies the realistic effect. The flesh tints of Nefert are buff, and of Ra-Hotep reddish-brown, a conventional mode of indicating that the skin of a man is generally darker than that of a woman, through greater exposure to the sun. The whites of the eyes are of quartz, and the pupils of crystal and perfectly transparent. The eyes were given greater brilliancy and intelligence by the insertion of pieces of silver back of the iris, producing an effect similar to that of the natural eye.

Another well-known statue, sometimes spoken of as the " Wooden Man of Bulak," or " Sheik-el-Beled," illustrates, to a remarkable degree, the realistic character of this early sculpture. This statue is considerably less than life-size, and represents Ra-en-ka, an overseer of public works. Unlike most statues of this early period, it is of wood, cut from the trunk of a tree that very likely waved its branches above the Nile banks more than fifty centuries ago.

From the tomb of Ti has been taken a number of portrait-statues. One of these, seven feet in height and sculptured from limestone, is now in the Cairo Museum. It was also customary to provide statues for the favorite servants of the deceased, in order that they might serve their masters as on earth. Therefore, we find statues of servants engaged in household tasks, also those of scribes or secretaries in the attitude of writing upon papyrus rolls. Not only in the serdabs of the early tombs do we find portrait-statues, but on the walls of the mastabas are exhibited pictorial compositions in low relief of most excellent workmanship.

STATUE OF SCRIBE: CAIRO MUSEUM

SPHINXES OF HYKSOS PERIOD: CAIRO MUSEUM

SCULPTURE. 217

Egyptian sculpture was formerly looked upon as a decidedly conventional art, but the discovery of the portrait-statues in the tombs of the Ancient Empire has revealed the fact that portrait-sculpture had attained perfection long before conventional types were adopted. Its origin and growth through long stages of development may never be known. We behold an art earlier than that of any other country, and yet one which, so far as we know, had reached maturity in the earliest period of recorded history. Although it may be traced back fully six thousand years, its infancy must have been of far greater antiquity than that period.

But after a long and remarkable period of development came an epoch known as that of the Hyksos rule, when little was done to foster art. These Semitic conquerors ruled Egypt, about two hundred years, till expelled by Aahmes, King of the XVIIIth Dynasty, about 1600 B. C. There have been found in the ruins of ancient Tanis couchant sphinxes having the bodies of lions and the faces of men. The faces of these figures are of an entirely different type from anything else found before or after the Hyksos period, and show, conclusively, foreign influence.

Again, in the period represented by Seti I. of the XIXth Dynasty, especially in the temple at Abydos erected by that great king, we find relief-sculpture approaching in beauty of execution that of the early period. The sculpture and inscriptions, except in the halls of later kings, are in low relief. The most careful workmanship has been given to every hieroglyphic character, to every figure of god and king, and to every line of decoration. Many of these forms show scarcely a trace of the long lapse of time, the cuttings being almost as clear and perfect as when first produced. What can convey more fully a knowledge of the art of that period and of one phase of the religious thought of the Egyptians, somewhat akin to that of Christian times, than the relief decoration of Abydos, representing Hathor, the divine mother, holding in her lap the divine child, Horus? How tender is the sentiment expressed! With what delicacy and grace of line is depicted every detail of dress and figure! How beautiful are the head-dress of the mother and

ISIS AND HORUS: TEMPLE OF ABYDOS

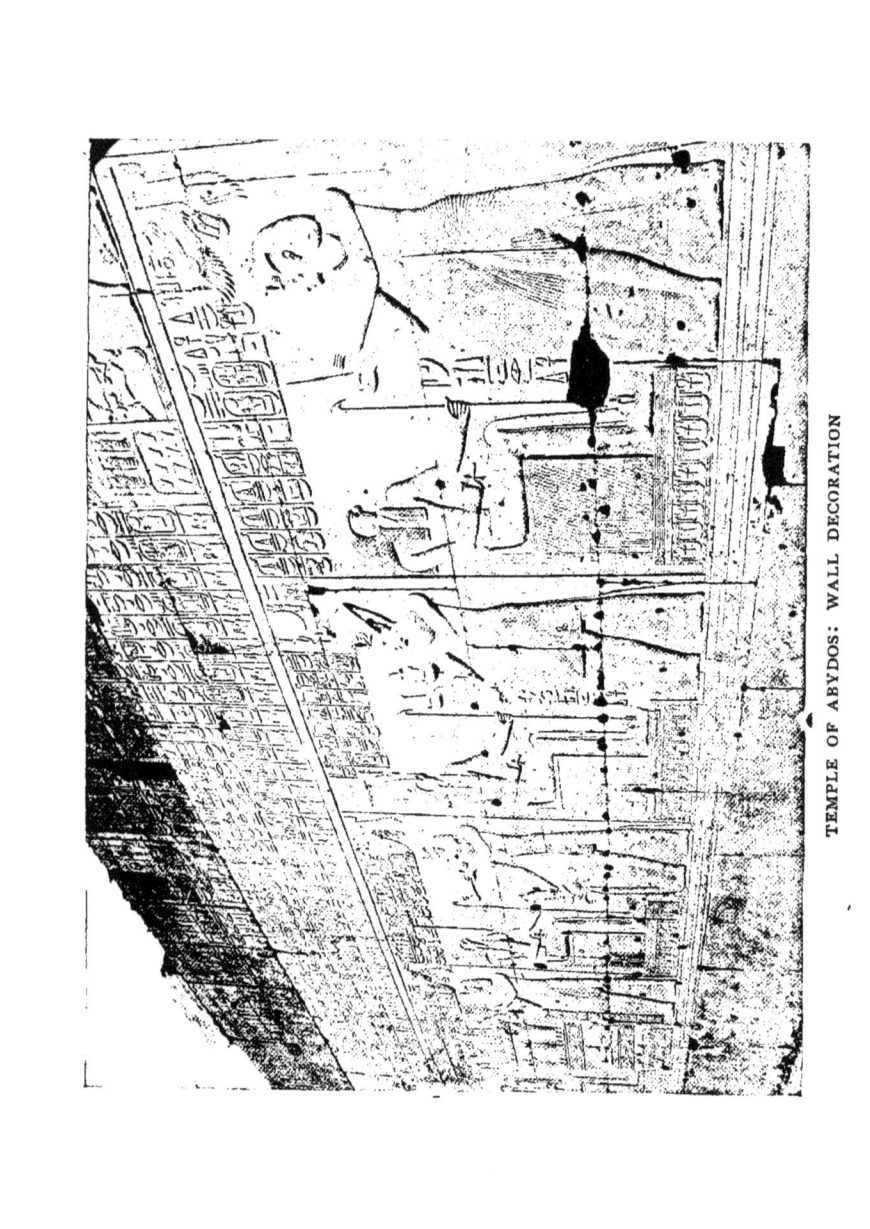

TEMPLE OF ABYDOS: WALL DECORATION

the necklace of the child! The throne-chair is decorated with a graceful lotus ornament representing the union of Upper and Lower Egypt, while the platform beneath the throne-chair has a border of pleasing design composed of the nilometer, the key of life, and the sceptre of power. The pictorial representation of food-offerings, with inscriptions relating to this sacred composition, is worked out with a nicety of detail that is almost incomprehensible.

This Memnonium of Seti I., at Abydos, was excavated, in 1853, by Mariette-Bey. It is not a religious temple in the same sense as are Karnak, Edfu, Denderah, and others, but is a sanctuary of the dead. The temple is upon the site of what is supposed to be one of the oldest cities of the Ancient Empire. It was looked upon as a holy city, famous for the grave of Osiris. Hither were brought the bodies of the dead for consecration in its holy sanctuary, and thrice blessed was he who was buried in its vicinity, for such a burial brought with it a favorable judgment in the future life. Men of power and authority directed that their mummies should receive the blessing of Osiris, at Abydos, before being interred among those of their ancestors.

Unlike that of most temples, the sanctuary consisted of seven chambers or chapels; seven being a sacred number. Each was dedicated to a different god; and one, to the reigning king, who in death would become united to Osiris. The chambers are roofed in imitation of the arch of heaven, and decorated with stars. The vaulted effect was obtained by cutting away the roofing-stones on the under side until a curved ceiling resulted. Without doubt, thousands of sacred memorial processions have passed through those chapel halls, the mummy being borne along through corridors and sanctuaries, making a complete circuit of the chapels. The hymns that were sung and the various ceremonies that were performed are illustrated by pictorial inscriptions. Amid solemn music and the perfume of burning incense, the ministering priests poured out wine offerings, and repeated prayers for the dead.

The decorations in the sanctuaries are remarkable for purity of style, for beauty of draughtsmanship and modelling, and for richness of color.

SANCTUARY: ABYDOS

TEMPLE OF ABYDOS: WALL DECORATION

The part of the temple built by Seti I. is noted for its wonderful relief-sculpture. Later decorations made under the direction of Rameses II., his son, are of a very different character, and mark the beginning of a decline in art.

The following inscription is of interest as showing the general character of Egyptian inscriptions upon temple walls, as well as the ambition and power of the great king, Rameses II.: "Then spoke His Majesty unto them and said: I summon you before me on account of a plan that has entered my mind. I have seen the buildings of the necropolis and the tombs that are at Abydos, and also those who have to work there. Truly nothing has been restored since the time of their lord unto the present day. But when a son finds himself on the throne of his father, shall he not renew the monument of his begetter? . . .

"I have called my father to a new life in gold [that is, as a statue] in the first year of my exaltation. I have given orders that his temple be adorned, and I have made sure his possession of the land. . . . I have offered him sacrifices. . . . And now, when his building stood in my power,

I watched over all the labors connected with it. ... I enlarged and renewed his palatial structure. I did not neglect his foundations, as wicked children do, who do not respect their father. I built new walls of the temple of my begetter. I presented before him the man whom I had selected to superintend the works. ... I erected pylons in front of it. ... I have covered his house with clothing [sculptures], I have adorned its columns, and provided stones for the foundations. A finished work was the monument, doubly as glorious as at first. It is named after my name and after the name of my father; for as the son, so is also the father."

Although, in the time of the New Empire, art regained much that had been lost by the rule of the Shepherd Kings, yet sculpture, compared with that of the Memphite period, became conventional in style. It was a time of conquest, and the kings took delight and satisfaction in erecting colossal statues typical of their power and commemorative of their deeds of prowess. Architecture also assumed enormous dimensions. Columns of prodigious size supported roofs of

STATUE OF RAMESES II : LUXOR

ABU-SIMBEL

vast halls. Great statues were placed in front of temples and between columns, to supplement other architectural features. The monolithic statue of Rameses II., in the temple of Luxor, the Colossus of the Ramesseum, fifty-seven feet in height and weighing nearly one thousand tons, the Colossi of Memnon, and the reclining statue of Rameses at Memphis are of this period. The temple tombs of Abu Simbel, cut into the solid rock, show four colossal relief figures of Rameses II., sixty-five feet high; and here, as elsewhere, the wife and children of the ruler are represented on a very small scale, and are placed at his feet. A relief of the god Ra, above the temple door, also is of insignificant proportions compared with the figure of the king.

The sphinx is another characteristic type of the sculpture of this second great period of Egyptian art. Sphinxes were placed in double rows along avenues leading to the temples, and, at Karnak, they were symbolic of the divine protection of Ammon-Ra, as is indicated by a small statue of the king standing between the paws under the head of each sphinx.

Unlike the earlier or Memphite period, representations of the deity in this period are many, and figures, statues, and small images are found everywhere. Statues of gods decorated the temple walls, but they did not equal in size the statues of the kings. Statuettes also occupied niches at the farther ends of the rooms in private dwellings, these niches corresponding to the sanctuary of the temple. Before these images were placed offerings of food and of flowers.

Naturally, the construction of large temples led to a deterioration in the representation of pictorial inscriptions. Larger wall-spaces were to be filled, and execution suffered in proportion to the size of the representation. The beautiful relief decorations of earlier times gave place to intaglio cutting, often roughly modelled. In a still later period known as the Renaissance, or Saitic, period, about six hundred years before Christ, we find a return to the use of small statues. These are often of bronze, and are of great beauty, being finished with much care and elegance.

AVENUE OF SPHINXES: KARNAK

TEMPLE OF EDFU: SHRINE WITHIN THE SANCTUARY

XIV.

TEMPLE DECORATION.

WE may think of the sanctuary of the very earliest temple as being simply a rectangular structure with four walls, probably of sun-dried brick. Later, these walls were built of stone and decorated with inscriptions. In further process of time, this single chamber became surrounded by other chambers, and all were enclosed by a high brick wall. Eventually, this outer wall was constructed of stone, and its façade carried up to a greater height than the rest of the temple, forming a magnificent and imposing pylon or gateway.

The Egyptian temple was not a place for public worship. It was not a place of gathering for prayer; few were admitted within its sacred precincts. It was a gift from the king, erected in order to secure favors from the gods. A certain uniformity of subject was followed in the pictorial representations that covered the temple. In almost every instance, the king is in the act of bestowing offerings upon, or asking favors of, divinities, who, in turn, respond by granting his prayers. In addition to pictures of gods and kings, the profuse decorations upon the walls and pylon include hieroglyphic inscriptions, telling of the king's gratitude and of his praise to the god of his fathers, interspersed with sacred symbols. Many of the decorations relate to sacred processions in which the king is leader. In these processions are carried the sacred emblems and images of the gods. The battle scenes, in which the king waged war for the protection of his people against the enemies of Egypt, and other deeds and exploits are portrayed. They were inscribed upon the walls primarily as a declaration of piety; but, between the lines, the modern student reads of the ambition of a powerful potentate, who desired to inform posterity of his superiority over the kings of other nations, his power over adversaries, and the benefits that he had bestowed upon his country and his people.

In the early period, the decorations in the

OFFERINGS TO OSIRIS: ABYDOS

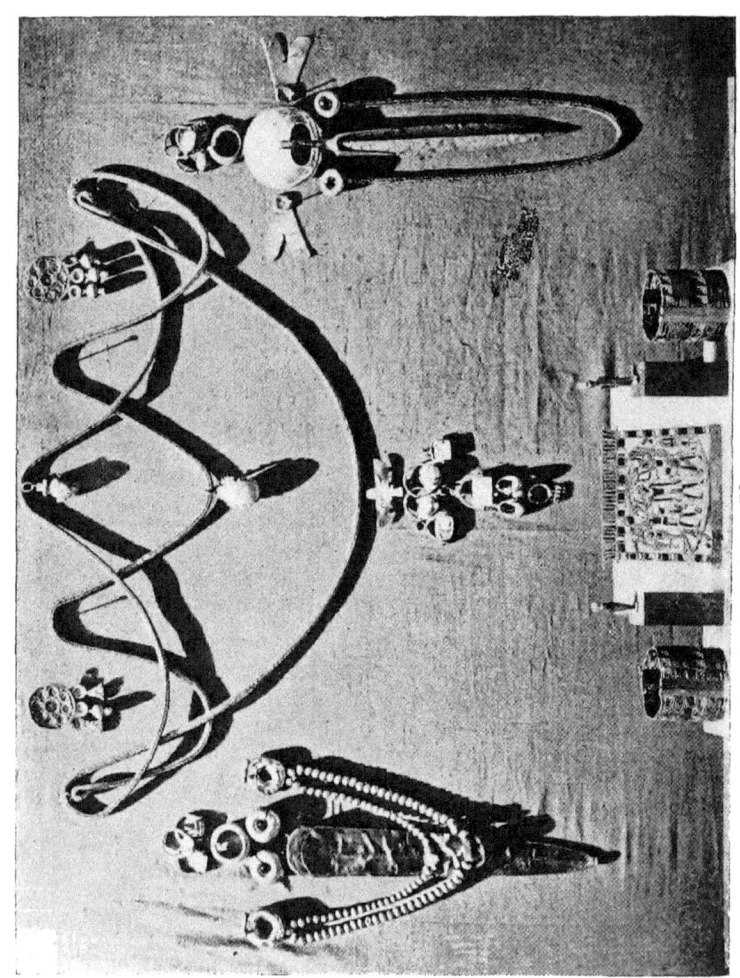

JEWELS OF QUEEN AAH-HOTEP, XVIIITH DYNASTY

tombs, as we have seen, concern man's earthly career and the things that would interest and benefit his Ka, which occupied the tomb. Worldly possessions, — all that had given wealth, comfort, and pleasure during life, — if pictured upon the tomb, were supposed to give pleasure and satisfaction to the Ka. In the later period, it will be remembered, the decorations relate to the afterlife, to the trials the soul was supposed to undergo after the spirit had left the body and before it had united with its god.

In all this pictorial decoration upon temple and tomb are found most beautiful drawings and relief ornaments. Over each doorway is carved the winged disk entwined with the two serpents. The drawing and modelling of this symbolic ornament are often marvellous. The sacred lotus-flower appears in every conceivable form of outline. It is represented in the bud, as the partly open flower, and as the full blossom upon the stalk. It is placed in the hands of kings; it forms a design about the shaft of columns, a border around the tomb-chamber, or the decoration on a throne-chair. In two different forms it symbolizes Upper and Lower Egypt. It decorates the capitals of columns, appearing as the bud and as the open flower. It is employed in gold ornaments, and is worn upon the body as an amulet. It is found upon mummy cases. Everywhere its sacred significance is apparent. It is the flower of the resurrection; the pure lily of the Nile, growing from its sacred waters, — the harbinger of coming plenty. The lotus symbol, appearing in thousands of drawings and in relief and color ornaments throughout Egypt, is often very beautifully executed, and illustrates the marvellous power of the Egyptians over line, a wonderful knowledge of proportion in design, and an exquisite sense of conventionalization. Most interesting drawings have been found in the tombs and temples, showing the gradual development of the lotus form from natural to conventional types; also the combination of the top view or rosette with the side view of the flower, producing what ultimately became the anthemion of Hellenic decoration.

It is evident that the Greeks got their first conception of the anthemion from the Egyptians;

SETI 1. MAKING OFFERINGS TO HORUS: KARNAK

TEMPLE OF EDFU: WALL DECORATION

perfecting the outline until it became the beautiful ornament one finds so often repeated on Greek vases and in architectural design. The winged disk, the lotus, and the scarabæus are the typical ornaments used in Egyptian decoration. Among other ornaments may be mentioned the nilometer (tat), — the symbol of steadfastness, — the key of life, the wave-scroll, and the zigzag. These not only appear singly, but are grouped in such a way as to produce very beautiful decorative designs.

Egyptian ornamentation serves a twofold purpose: beneath the representation is a beautiful spiritual thought, the expression of which never hampered the artist. He possessed the skill and the artistic instinct by means of which he was able to combine religious symbols in decorative compositions, producing perfect harmony of effect.

The Egyptians not only drew plant forms with skill and beauty, but also represented animals and birds with wonderful accuracy and detail. Especially is this true of the art of the Ancient Empire, as is illustrated by the decorations in the tombs dating back three thousand years before Christ.

It seems very strange that a people who could draw animals, birds, and flowers with such accuracy and beauty of line both in relief and in color, should have represented the human figure in such a conventional manner, violating laws of anatomy and oftentimes approaching the grotesque. Only in the sculpture of the very early period, at the time of the pyramid-builders, do we find a successful attempt at realistic portraiture, and a near approach to true proportions and correct anatomical rendering. Between the pictorial representation of the human form and that of animal and plant life there is a wide differentiation in correctness of expression.

In the three best periods of Egyptian art, approximately 3000 B. C., 2000 B. C. and 1500 B. C., ornaments, pictures, and inscriptions were modelled in low relief and afterwards colored. In later decorations, the work was intaglio in character; all pictorial forms being modelled slightly between the outlines, and the highest surface made flush with the face of the wall. This was a more

HUNTING SCENE: MEDINET-ABU

WALL DECORATION: TOMB OF NAKHT

TEMPLE DECORATION.

expeditious method of carving, but less artistic results were obtained.

The sculptor was followed in his work by the painter. Black, reddish-brown, pale brown, yellow, light and dark blue, and green were the colors generally employed. Egyptian women were always represented with pale yellow complexions; men, with reddish-brown skin. The unpainted stone indicated white. Blue was used for iron; yellow or red, for bronze; brown, for wood. Plant forms received colors strikingly different from those of nature, while animals were given more natural coloring.

While it is difficult to define the purpose of all the decorations of the Egyptian temple, it is clear that their arrangement was not accidental, but that both method and sequence existed in their plan, and much symbolism in their composition. There is evidence that the Egyptians, in building their temples, intended to reproduce, in a measure, the world in which they lived but of which they had only a limited conception. The wonderfully clear sky of the rainless regions of the Nile was bright with the golden sun by day and with myriads of stars by night. The horizon-line swept round without obstruction and divided the earth from the magnificent vault of the heavens. Astronomy was a favorite study, and all elements in nature had a religious significance. It was but natural that the floor of the temple should be made to correspond to the earth, while the ceiling should represent the sky. Not entirely satisfied with a flat ceiling, the Egyptians attempted to imitate the celestial arch, studding its blue ground with the stars and constellations. The lower part of the temple wall was decorated with plant forms, while between the floor and the ceiling, or, as it were, between earth and heaven, were pictured scenes illustrating the relationship of men to the gods. Here were portrayed the sacrificial scenes in which the king played the important part; for he alone could enter into close communion with the gods, and, through him, man came into touch with the divine. As the temple symbolized the universe, all the gods were represented, although each temple was specially dedicated to some one god or triad of gods. The lesser gods assisted in

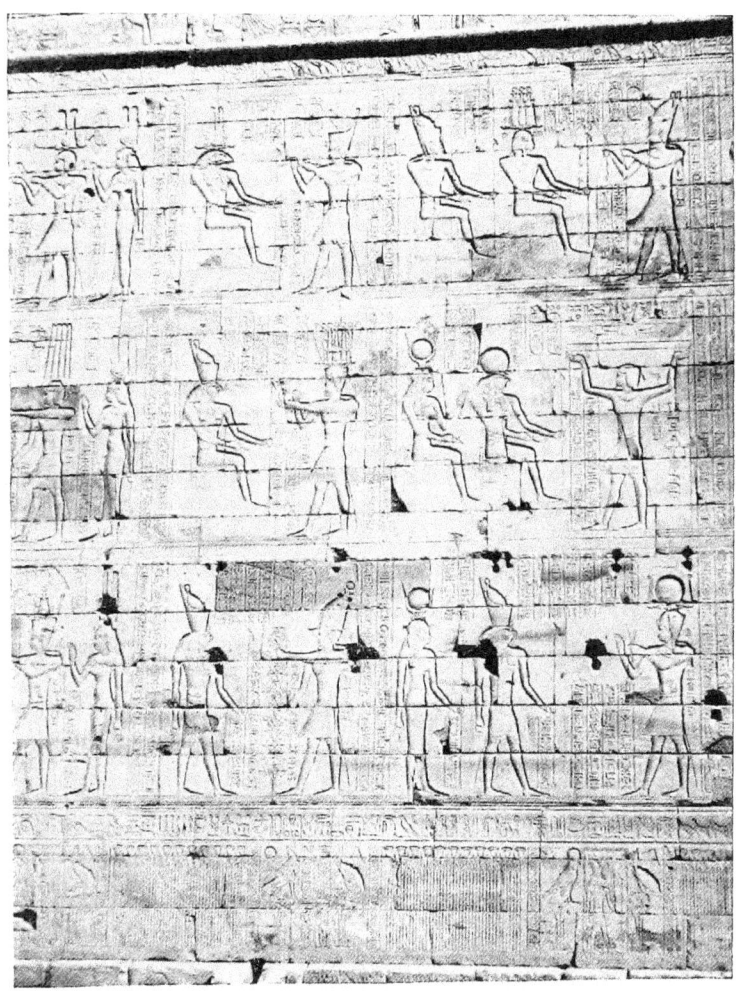

TEMPLE OF EDFU: WALL DECORATION

PYRAMID AND NATIVE VILLAGE

the religious services. Symbolism was everywhere apparent, color was freely employed, especially upon the ceiling and other interior surfaces. As the Egyptians probably derived from nature the thought regarding the construction of their temples and their symbolic decorations, so, without doubt, were they influenced by their environment in the use of color.

No day in their country closes without its glorious sunset. The great ball of fire drops into the sand of the Libyan desert; the river becomes a field of magnificent color; palm-groves are silhouetted against the sky; strange outlines are seen here and there; the women go to the river to fill their water-jars; weird forms hurry to and fro; darkness comes on quickly; then, suddenly, the wonderful after-glow streams up from the western horizon. The heavens become a play of color. It is like a sudden glorious transformation from the realities of life into the ideal surroundings of another world, beautiful beyond description. Then the color fades away; darkness comes rapidly: it is night, and all is quiet upon the dark shores of the River Nile.

XV.
THE APPLIED ARTS.

THE ancient Egyptians had a most remarkable appreciation of the laws governing architecture; of the principles of composition and design; of color in relation to environment and light; and of the crafts in stone, metal, wood, textiles, gold, and semi-precious stones.

In their architecture the strong vertical lines of the massive temples were in keeping with the lines of the cliffs and palms that formed an ever-present landscape background. The long horizontal lines of roofs and lintels repeated with exquisite harmony the broad stretches of fertile soil and barren desert. No architecture that has since developed would be so well adapted to the land of the Nile and the cliffs of the surrounding desert. No other people have more truly related their architecture to its environment. Believing implicitly in the resurrection and everlasting life, their architecture is sym-

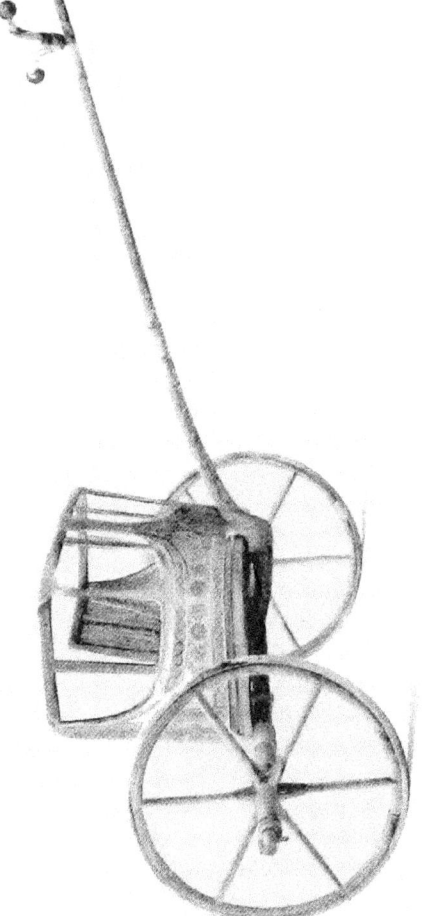

CHARIOT. TOMB OF IOUIYA AND TOUIYOU

TEMPLE OF DER-EL-BAHRI: WALL DECORATION

bolic of the permanence of their doctrines, of the majesty of their gods, and of their deep faith in the divine powers of nature. Egyptian art is absolutely true to nature and to the principles that govern good design.

In a country of brilliant sunlight and of strong contrasts between the verdure of the narrow river bed and the sterile desert sands and glistening cliffs, color was absolutely essential to decoration. This intensity of light necessitated walls without many openings. The various rooms were lighted by apertures in the roof or walls that were only a few inches in measurement.

The walls of the temple rooms were like open books, covered as they were with the decorative picture language relating to the divine service of the temple and the deeds of the gods and kings. This picture language was in low relief, calling for the greatest skill of the sculptor. This low relief sculpture would have lost its real value in the darkened chambers if it had not been covered with color. The painter, therefore, followed the sculptor, and by the addition of color produced a rich interior. The tombs of the early periods were decorated in the same way. In the later periods the walls of the tombs were sometimes covered with stucco and the scenes painted directly upon the flat surfaces. The brilliancy of the sunshine rendered necessary strong contrasts of color. These were softened in appearance to the eye by intensity of light in the open and by dullness of light in the interior.

The work of the best periods of Egyptian art required great skill on the part of the artist. The drawing of animals, flower forms, and designs was wonderfully accurate and the modeling was beautiful in its delicate relief. It was necessary then, as to-day, to have schools for the training of young artists to fill the places of the older sculptors and painters. Each artist may have had a number of apprentices or assistants who learned the profession by aiding the master workman.

As stated elsewhere, the earliest sculpture that we know is very realistic. Before, and at the time of the pyramid builders, it had reached a wonderful perfection in the round and in portraiture. At no time subsequent to this early period do we find any approach to such vitality and strength of individualism. The diorite statue

WALL DECORATION. TOMB OF SETI I.

MUMMY CASES. CAIRO MUSEUM

THE APPLIED ARTS. 257

of Chephren, the builder of the second pyramid, is a magnificent example of the sculptor's art of that very ancient period.

Undoubtedly painting as an art came before sculpture, but as it is more perishable we have no examples of the earliest periods. The great period of Egyptian painting was between 1600 B. C. and 1200 B. C., when sculpture in relief was largely given up in favor of a more delicate and expeditious treatment of surface decoration. During this period painting reached a high degree of development. The mural compositions that cover the temples and tombs acquaint us with the life of the people to an astonishing degree of realism. The industrial life, as carried on in the cultivation of the fields, hunting, fishing, the preparation of food, as well as the amusements of daily life, are depicted with such skill in execution and in the use of color, as to make us acquainted with that free home and village life not usually associated with the ancient Egyptian and his art because of unfortunate errors in historical writing. The vast numbers of pictures found in tombs and temples exhibit wonderful facility in drawing and keen appreciation of the principles that govern decorative composition.

In the crafts the Egyptians displayed the same ability as in the decorative arts. In the predynastic age the hardest and finest stone, including basalt, porphyry, and syenite were used. Later limestone, alabaster and other soft stones became popular. As time advanced, there was a decline both in the quality of stone used and in workmanship.

In the prehistoric age flint instruments reached a state of perfection unknown outside of Egypt. Flint knives were made with teeth so fine as to be almost imperceptible to the eye. Bracelets of flint of most extraordinary thinness display the remarkable workmanship of the time and the desire for beautiful and refined ornaments. Work of this quality in flint is now entirely a lost art.

Beads, also, were used in prehistoric times. These were often made of quartz, amethyst, agate, carnelian, turquoise and lapis lazuli. Vases of remarkable form and contour were cut from hard stone and hollowed out to an extreme thinness of material.

COUCH. TOMB OF IOUIYA AND TOUIYOU

COFFER TOMB OF IOUIYA AND TOUIYOU

Gold was also employed in the earliest times, even in the predynastic periods. Necklaces, bracelets, anklets, rings, and other objects of personal adornment in gold and semi-precious stones, as illustrated on page 236, were used extensively throughout the centuries of Egyptian art. Many of those ornaments are as beautifully executed as ornaments of the present day. Indeed, the gold jewelry of the best periods is superb in design, workmanship and fitness to purpose. When it is considered how many tombs must have been robbed of their contents, the great amount of jewelry left undiscovered till modern times is an indication of the wealth prevailing in the periods named.

Among the metals used for other than ornamental purposes, we find that copper was mined and worked in periods much further back in time than the building of the pyramids. The copper vessels were shaped by hammering. Polished stone hammers were employed, but without handles.

Bronze came into general use about sixteen hundred years before Christ, and objects were usually cast in bronze in the most approved method of the present day. This was done first by modeling the object in wax over a hard core of sand. The wax model was then covered with a mold, the wax melted out, and the bronze poured into the space between the mold and the inner core. Seven hundred years before Christ copper work was decorated by inlaying gold and silver lines to form a design, a method used in the far East to-day. Although iron was used at least three thousand years before Christ, it did not come into general use until about 800 B. C.

Glazed ware has been used in Egypt for thousands of years. Glaze in color was first employed on objects made of stone, although blue and green beads of glazed clay, made up into necklaces, date back to the earliest known periods. Innumerable figures of gods, men, and animals in glazed silica have been found belonging to the various historic periods. Sixteen hundred to thirteen hundred years before Christ was the great period of glazed ware produced in many colors. There were shades of viel and green amulst e o ds, te s, or ns and t o e s. c h a s, war mspen hnr, and mb ma- en s for ne k a es e e a e in a ge n e s.

Glass dates from about 1500 B. C., beads being

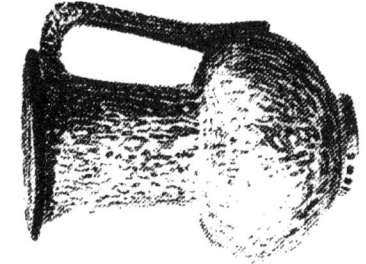

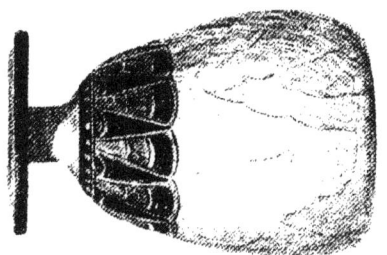

PAINTED VASES. TOMB OF IOUIYA AND TOUIYOU

PAINTED WOODEN BOXES TOMB OF IOUIYA AND TOUIYOU

THE APPLIED ARTS. 265

made in various colors. Blown glass, however, was not known in Egypt till about the time of Christ. Ivory work was one of the early applied arts, being done with fine spirit and individuality.

Pottery has always been a special feature of Egyptian crafts work. A great many jars or fragments of jars of various shapes have been excavated, many dating back to a prehistoric age. Color to enrich the various designs was employed throughout the ages of pottery making.

Wood is now very scarce in Egypt, but there is evidence that in early times it was used freely, even in building. The great gates of the temples and palaces must have been of wood and beautifully decorated. Some of these gates in pairs were thirty feet wide and fifty to sixty feet high. Even to-day the thresholds of some of the temples of Egypt show where they were worn by the gates that swung upon hinges, there being holes several inches deep that received the pivots in which the hinges of the doors were hung.

Immense numbers of wooden coffins were used and these were elaborately decorated in color. The tombs of the period from 1600 to 1200 B. C.

have revealed most beautiful furniture, that was placed in the tomb with the mummy. This furniture is most remarkable in design and workmanship. Chairs were carved as elaborately as in the present day. The seats of the chairs were sometimes covered with woven material, and supplied with cushions filled with goose feathers. A couch such as seen in the illustration is of graceful design, while the coffer, which is one of several found, is most elaborate in its decoration of color and inlaid work.

The furniture was braced and strengthened by angle pieces made of wood with bent grain, and by diagonal bars. The backs of large chairs were supported by a triangular brace and the panelling was constructed with special attention to strength and to excellence in design. The tomb of Iouiya and Touiyou, discovered in 1905, contained many beautiful pieces of furniture. In another tomb a chariot has been found of exquisite proportions and beauty of decorative design.

Linen was used in the earliest periods, even as early as 4000 B. C. It is of excellent weave, employing nearly one hundred and fifty threads to

CHAIR TOMB OF IOUIYA AND TOUIYOU

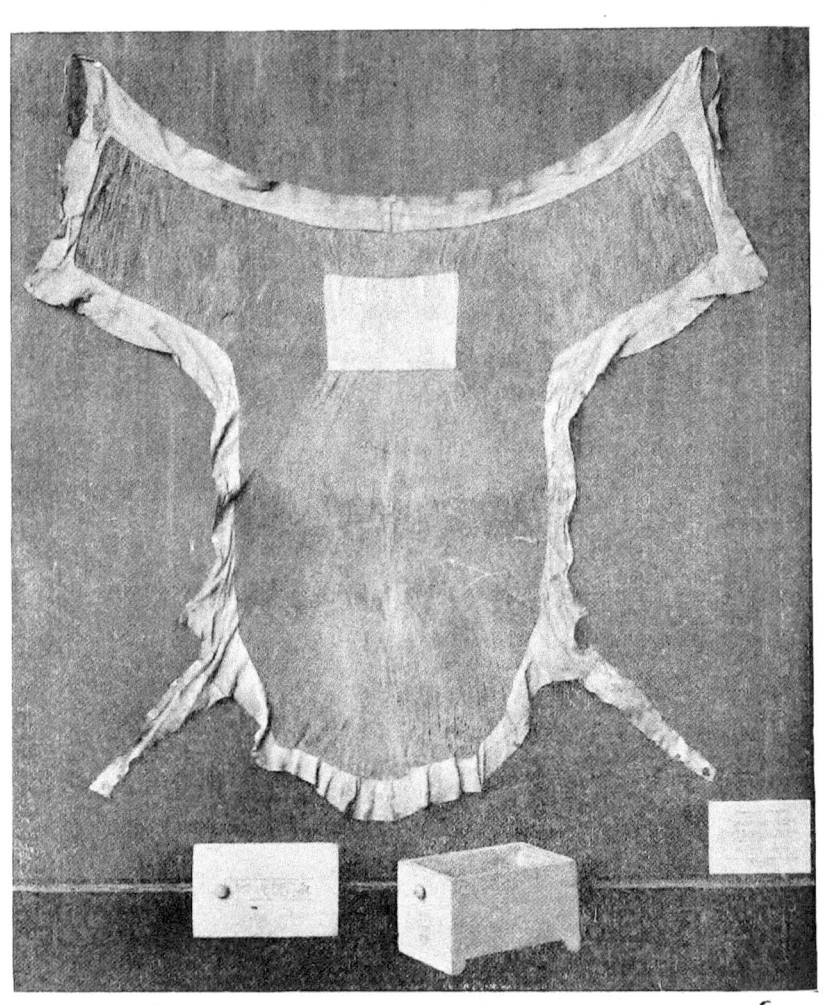
CEREMONIAL ROBE: BOSTON MUSEUM

the inch. The hand-work of this very early period quite equals the work of the present day in quality and fineness of execution. The cloth preserved to us of the early periods was employed for mummy wrappings, and this, fine as it is, can not be equal to the best woven fabrics that were used for clothing. Pieces of mummy cloth have been found five feet and more in width and fifty feet in length, showing that the looms must have been large and adaptable.

Leather work was always an important craft in ancient Egypt. Appliqué work in colors was quite common. Leather was also cut so as to be pulled out into wide meshes. This required great skill in the use of the knife. Rows of slits were cut so that the joints would break one with another. No finer specimen of this leather cutting has been found than the gazelle-skin garment now in the Boston Museum and here illustrated. The garment was found in a small wooden box in a tomb of the XVIIIth Dynasty. It belonged to a prince who was a cup-bearer of Thothmes IV., a king who reigned about 1430 B. C.

To the Egyptians art was the most exalted

medium through which to express their loftiest thoughts. Through it they addressed their gods, proclaimed their religion, and portrayed life. It being characteristic of the Egyptian to conserve everything he created, the crafts formed a most vital, tangible means through which to perpetuate material representations of doctrinal beliefs, superstitious notions, and religious devices for serving the soul after death. Hence all the crafts reached a high state of development.

Through art the ancient Egyptians communicated emotions high, noble and sincere; magnificent in stability and strength; imposing in sincerity of utterance. They conquered the resisting powers of the hardest stone, transforming it into imperishable monuments, superb in their dignity and beauty, and absolutely obedient to the laws of art in nature. From the least unto the greatest, their art is a glowing tribute to sincerity and truth.

www.ingramcontent.com/pod-product-compliance
Lightning Source LLC
Chambersburg PA
CBHW061247230426
43663CB00021B/2934